Edward B. Segel

New European Orders, 1919 and 1991

New European Orders, 1919 and 1991

Edited by
Samuel F. Wells, Jr.
Paula Bailey Smith

W Published by *The Woodrow Wilson Center Press*
Distributed by *The Johns Hopkins University Press*

Woodrow Wilson Center Special Studies

The Woodrow Wilson Center Press
Editorial Offices
370 L'Enfant Promenade, S.W.
Suite 704
Washington, D.C. 20024-2518 U.S.A.
telephone 202-287-3000, ext. 218

Distributed by
The Johns Hopkins University Press
Hampden Station
Baltimore, Maryland 21211
order department telephone 1-800-537-5487

9 8 7 6 5 4 3 2 1

Library of Congress Cataloging-in-Publication Data

New European orders, 1919 and 1991 / edited by Samuel F. Wells, Jr. and Paula
  Bailey Smith.
    p.   cm. — (Woodrow Wilson Center special studies)
    Includes bibliographical references and index.
    ISBN 0-943875-76-5. — ISBN 0-943875-77-3 (pbk.)
    1. Europe—Politics and government—1989–   2. World War, 1914–1918—
Influence. 3. World War, 1914–1918—Peace. I. Wells, Samuel F.   II. Smith,
Paula Bailey.   III. Series.
D2009.N495   1996   96-16791
327'.094'0904—dc20   CIP

The Woodrow Wilson International Center for Scholars

The Center is the living memorial of the United States of America to the nation's twenty-eighth president, Woodrow Wilson. Congress established the Woodrow Wilson Center in 1968 as an international institute for advanced study, "symbolizing and strengthening the fruitful relationship between the world of learning and the world of public affairs." The Center opened in 1970 under its own board of trustees.

Woodrow Wilson Center Special Studies

The work of the Center's Fellows, Guest Scholars, and staff—and presentations and discussions at the Center's conferences, seminars, and colloquia—often deserve timely circulation as contributions to public understanding of issues of national and international importance. The Woodrow Wilson Center Special Studies series is intended to make such materials available by the Woodrow Wilson Center Press to interested scholars, practitioners, and other readers. In all its activities, the Woodrow Wilson Center is a nonprofit, nonpartisan organization, supported financially by annual appropriations from the U.S. Congress, and by the contributions of foundations, corporations, and individuals. Conclusions or opinions expressed in Center publications and programs are those of the authors and speakers and do not necessarily reflect the views of the Center staff, Fellows, trustees, advisory groups, or any individuals or organizations that provide financial support to the Center.

Contents

Acknowledgments

This book originated in two conferences cosponsored by the East and West European Studies Program of the Woodrow Wilson International Center for Scholars. The first was held in Washington, D.C., in March 1993 and was made possible by support from Federal Conference Funds granted to the Woodrow Wilson Center. The second was held at the Central European University in Prague, Czech Republic, in June 1993 with support from Federal Conference Funds and the Open Society Funds of the Soros Foundation.

The editors gratefully acknowledge the contributions of John R. Lampe, director, East European Studies, to the design and proceedings of the conferences, and to the content of the final manuscript, and Kristin Hunter, program assistant, East European Studies.

Introduction

Samuel F. Wells, Jr.

In the months after the opening of the Berlin Wall in November 1989, policymakers and specialists watched the rapid flow of events with pleasure and awe as country after country threw off repressive governments and institutions and opted for freedom. In the euphoria of seeing Eastern Europe reject forty-five years of communism and prior centuries of authoritarian rule, analysts searched for parallels to guide policy reactions and shape thinking. Some drew comparisons with the wave of liberal revolutions that swept across Europe in 1848. Others saw an analogy with the renewal and reconstruction that followed the end of World War II and proposed the Marshall Plan as the model for Western guidance. A few, including the authors of this volume, examined the problems of economic reconstruction, nationalism, and ethnic conflict and saw parallels with the end of World War I. In order to focus on the complex interrelated problems of the 1990s, many of which had roots in the era of the Versailles conference of 1919, we chose to focus this volume on a sustained comparison of the end of World War I and the end of the cold war.

The dates 1919 and 1991 were chosen as symbols of their eras. Beyond numerology, they both have significance. Better than any other year, 1919 with the pageantry and drama of the Versailles

conference and the major U.S. role in shaping the peace sym-
bolizes the post–World War I order. The year 1991 is less inclu-
sive of all the trends we want to explore, but it saw many events
critical to the shaping of a post–cold war order. The Soviet parliament ratified the Treaty of German Unification in March. After
Croatia and Slovenia declared independence in June, Yugoslavia
broke apart and civil war began. The coup against Mikhail Gorbachev occurred in August followed by declarations of independence by the Baltic republics, Ukraine, and other republics
of the Soviet Union. In December the Soviet Union dissolved,
while the twelve nations of the European Union signed the
Maastricht Treaty pledging economic and political union. As our
authors examine the events of these years, in each case they will
compare developments that span several years before and after
the focal dates of 1919 and 1991.

Historical analogies are attractive to authors and can be useful,
yet they invariably contain the seeds of misperception and mis-
representation within them. A good analogy can show the origins and suggest aspects of a problem that may not be obvious,
as in the case of Ernest May's superb essay that examines the
roles of public opinion, expert advisers, and the news media in
shaping the peace of 1919 and compares this situation with the
settlement in 1991. By showing how important mass and expert
opinion were in 1919, as well as the immense power of colum-
nists like Walter Lippmann and publishers like Lord Beaverbrook in England, May points out the absence of similar
influences in 1991. Despite today's instant global communication
and what we refer to as the "CNN phenomenon," media and expert opinion had less influence at the end of the cold war. This
is largely because governments have taken experts and public
relations specialists inside and now use them to shape policy and
mold opinion—or, in contemporary journalistic jargon, to give
"spin" to an issue.

Analogies can also create misleading comparisons and help to
generate false expectations. Recall how many times after 1989
one heard that the United States and its allies "had won the cold
war" and that we could expect a quick transition to free institutions, meaning a democratic political system and a market economy. Yet the collapse of the Soviet Empire in 1989 and the
dissolution of the Soviet Union in 1991 were not the same as the
defeat of the German and Austro-Hungarian Empires in 1918.

When compared with the defeat of 1945, the German armistice in 1918 was not so clear a defeat that it prevented potent arguments about internal betrayal of the army and a stab in the back. But 1989–91 was even less clear as a defeat compared with 1918–19. Although communism failed and was discredited in 1989, the Western system did not automatically extend to the East. This created two very large problems. Our false expectations prevented us from realizing the need for early integration of the countries of Eastern Europe into Western institutions because the West assumed that its system had been accepted by the former captive countries of the Warsaw Pact and would automatically spread to the East. Second, we lacked any adequate understanding of how difficult both economic and political transitions would be in countries that had for decades been under centralized rule and significant foreign domination.

Among other highlights in the volume, John Ikenberry compares the postwar settlements in 1815, 1919, and 1945 with problems at the end of the cold war. He examines issues of state interests, domestic political coalitions, and legitimacy in new international regimes. Ernest May shows how a lack of competition from prominent exiles, issue experts, and news media specialists in 1991 allowed officials to dominate policy choices in a way that they could not approach in 1919.

Michael Burns examines the revival of nationalism and its role in ethnic conflicts in 1919 and after 1989. He shows how nationalism has posed large problems for international institutions and principles. Limits must be placed on self-determination, he argues, to prevent a vast number of microstates from being created and many episodes of ethnic cleansing from occurring. Steven Burg looks at some of the lessons from the Yugoslav crisis and proposes the creation of international standards of human rights and shared sovereignty, conditions that would be imposed before diplomatic recognition of new states created by border changes.

Charles Maier examines in depth the economic problems facing national leaders and international regimes at the end of World War I and at the end of the cold war. He points out that socialist economic policies during the cold war created distortions and inefficient patterns of production that probably destroyed as much economic potential as did two world wars. Despite this level of economic dislocation, the industrial nations have not approached this problem with the same level of aid or a coordinated regional program that would be essential to deal with economic problems successfully before political backlash sets in. Maier also questions whether "transition" is a suitable concept for analysis. The East European economies may not be capable of becoming like those of Western Europe, and transition toward a Western model may not be the right way to think about their changes. Indeed, we must realize that the West European economies are well on the road to something very different as they adapt to postindustrial economic conditions with a limited manufacturing sector, large service industries, and sustained high unemployment.

David Dilks examines a range of security problems that have vastly changed since 1919. He describes the flawed system of collective security created around the League of Nations at the Versailles conference and shows how its internal contradictions were severely damaging and how the system was made unworkable by the refusal of the United States to participate. He points out the dramatically different situations of the 1990s due in large part to the existence of two highly successful multinational institutions: the European Union and the North Atlantic Treaty Organization (NATO). The problems of the 1990s, he argues, are much more suited to a strengthened form of collective security with full U.S. participation than to the type of NATO-based collective defense that successfully integrated Germany into the West and waged the cold war.

The essays that follow do not provide a road map for the new international order that will follow the cold war. They do highlight a range of interesting comparisons through twentieth-century history up to our own day, and they provide a number of cautionary arguments against assuming that the future will be totally different from the past and that its course will be easy and linear.

Chapter 1

Political Structures and Postwar Settlements

G. John Ikenberry

In the modern era, great wars have periodically left the relations of states in ruins. In the aftermath of these upheavals, leaders of the major states have sought to put the pieces of interstate relations back together in order to create a new international order. These large-scale attempts to build order have taken shape in the process of arriving at postwar settlements. After the Napoleonic wars of the nineteenth century and again after the two world wars in the twentieth century, the Great Powers negotiated the terms of peace and, in doing so, grappled with the problems of creating order. Many observers now argue that with the end of the cold war, the major powers are again searching for a new postwar settlement.

The major postwar settlements have all attempted to deal with the full range of problems brought on by war, including reparations, territorial settlements, and reconstruction. But they have also sought to forge agreement over the basic rules and institutions of the postwar order. Historian Gordon Craig and political scientist Alexander George have argued that the Vienna settlement was, in effect, an effort to craft a "constitution" for Great Power relations.[1] Although the outcomes differed, the settlements of 1919 and 1945 were no less ambitious.

The basic question raised by these settlements is how disorder is turned into order. How is the basic governance of the international system reestablished after major war and upheaval? If order is something that is built, are there properties or laws of architecture, design, and construction that constrain and direct all the major historical efforts at interstate order building? If state leaders seek to establish an international order that is legitimate and will endure, what are the conditions that foster legitimacy and durability? Many people are speculating on the shape of the new European and world order. The question here is less frequently asked: How is order created?

In examining the character and logic of past settlements, we are in a position to draw connections with the present. There is reason to think that the current search for a post–cold war settlement resembles the efforts of the previous postwar junctures of 1815, 1919, and 1945. Then, as now, the old order was overturned by dramatic shifts in the fortunes of major states. Then, as now, the relations among the Great Powers were at a crossroads, and the basic rules and institutions that governed the system were called into question. As at these earlier junctures, the world's major states are once again presented with a historical "opening," an unusual and fleeting opportunity to shape the basic features of the international system.

The experiences of 1815, 1919, and 1945 tell us that postwar settlements are more than the redrawing of the balance of power, with the victors simply dictating the terms of the peace. These settlements are multifaceted events in which power realities mix with the evolving norms of order, the domestic politics of the leading states, and the specific historical vagaries of the postwar situation in shaping the outcome. The discrediting of the old order, the changed power relations among states, the states' own internal instability, and the pervasive uncertainty surrounding future interstate relations make the postwar search for order an extremely complex process, the success of which depends on the leaders' ability to craft a settlement that is acceptable to both the winners and the losers.

Today's leaders can learn from these earlier experiments in postwar order formation. Although not involving the same collapse of the security, political, or economic order that left the peacemakers of 1815, 1919, and 1945 little choice but to attempt to construct new rules and institutions, the change ushered in by the end of the cold war is nevertheless problematic. Like their predecessors, the Western leaders of today are confronted by the question of how best to reintegrate a group of "defeated" states into the Western system. It is in this respect that the lessons of earlier postwar settlements, lessons about mistakes as well as successes, are most powerful. This essay focuses on the characteristics of postwar settlements and explores the conditions that lie behind the successful creation of order.

What Are Postwar Settlements?

Change in the organization of states has always been irregular and episodic, and war has often been its agent. The importance of armed conflict, breakdown, and reconstruction to the major efforts to build basic rules and institutions speaks to a central aspect of international change, namely, that history is, as political scientist Peter Katzenstein has suggested, a "sequence of irregular big bangs."[2] It is marked by infrequent discontinuities that rearrange world politics.

The major postwar settlements were all culminations of historical "big bangs." At the Congress of Vienna in 1815 following the Napoleonic wars, European leaders reached agreement on territorial and security relations, agreements that lasted a generation. Most important, Prince Klemens Wenzel von Metternich, Czar Alexander I, and Robert Stewart, Viscount Castlereagh, agreed that the international order had to be managed by a consultative process. After World War I, there was a bold effort to build a new international order, but that effort ended in bitter failure. Although the United States advanced the most far-reaching proposals, its leaders were unable to generate sufficient domestic support to ratify the agreement. Meanwhile, Britain and France, whose leaders were profoundly influenced by nineteenth-century European history, had very different conceptions of what constituted a desirable postwar order. By contrast, in the aftermath of World War II, Western leaders were able to set aside their differences and create institutions that reopened the world economy and united the industrial democracies in a security alliance.[3]

These shifts in the system are what political scientist Robert Gilpin calls "systemic change," moments when the governing rules and institutions are remade to suit the interests of the newly powerful states or hegemon.[4] This type of change is fundamentally different from either "systems change," which is change in the basic character of the actors within the global system, or "interaction change," which is change in the political and economic processes among actors. Systemic change is distinctive in that it involves efforts to redefine and reestablish interstate governance arrangements. Power realities have changed, often as a result of war, and basic rules and institutions must be redrawn. These are the great transitional moments in international relations. The old order has broken down, a new distribution of power between states has arisen, and multiple courses of action are possible. The struggle to shape the new order unfolds during the negotiations over the postwar settlement. Postwar settlements tend to focus on three issues: territorial and economic restitution, reintegration of defeated states, and creation of new rules and institutions.

The peace conferences of 1815, 1919, and 1945 were primarily concerned with the settlement of political, territorial, and financial claims arising from war. These settlements generally took the form of treaties—documents that became increasingly lengthy and complicated with each war. The settlement following the Napoleonic wars was embodied in a single treaty. The 1919 settlement required the conclusion of one major treaty and four subsidiary treaties. While dealing with familiar matters such as indemnity and restitution, the 1919 documents also introduced subjects such as railroad and aerial navigation. Most important, at the insistence of U.S. President Woodrow Wilson, the Versailles treaty contained the text of the Covenant of the League of Nations. The settlement of 1945, which was even more elaborate, required three major and five minor treaties. Although these treaties did not contain the equivalent of the League of Nations text, they did include new political clauses on both human rights and the effects of the internal structures of defeated states on individuals within those states.[5]

The second great question that these settlements addressed was the reintegration of the defeated states into the postwar order.[6] The settlements of 1815 and 1945 resulted in a "generous peace," in which the defeated states were rehabilitated and were returned, in various degrees, to their earlier major power status. In 1815 this was accomplished partly by design but also because of the persistence and diplomatic skill of Charles-Maurice de Talleyrand-Perigord, whose manipulations succeeded in restoring France's position in the Great Power club. In 1945 the reintegration was accomplished with much more intensive and systematic intervention by the Western allies to reform the domestic political and economic institutions of Germany and Japan. In 1919, despite resistance at various moments from American and British officials both before and after the Paris Peace Conference, negotiations resulted in a punitive peace. Of Germany's 1910 territory, 13 percent was confiscated, and the Germans were prohibited from joining the League of Nations. Moreover, in sharp contrast with the peacemaking of 1815, the German representatives in 1919 were simply handed the terms of the peace rather than invited to participate in the drafting.

The final task of the major postwar settlements has been to define and reestablish international rules and institutions. Re-creating the security order has always been paramount in these settlements, but in the twentieth century, economic rules and institutions became increasingly important as well. In 1815 the diplomats in Vienna produced an elaborate structure of security agreements that resulted in a concert-of-power system among the Great Powers. In 1919 the League of Nations was the institutional expression of the principles of self-determination, arms control, and economic and social cooperation. In 1945 the rules and institutions were more diffuse, although the United Nations and the Bretton Woods agreements did provide an overall framework for the postwar order. In each case, rule making and institution building were accomplished in difficult and sometimes scattered diplomatic negotiations.

These are the complex and interconnected areas of activity that are the heart of postwar settlements. To think of these settlements as "constitutional" in nature may require some imagination, but in a primitive way they surely were. Basic principles and expectations were generated in these settings; the "big bang" of history was given some predictable shape.

Power versus Problem Solving

The traditional way in which to view postwar settlements is through the lens of realist theory, which emphasizes the centrality of hegemony and the balance of power. In general, realists believe that agreements and institutions are produced by and reflect state power. Some realists argue that order is produced by the persistent struggle of individual states to balance the power of other states.[7] Thus, order is the result of the successful adjustment of states to the underlying distribution of power. Other realists argue that order is created and maintained by the most powerful—that is, hegemonic—states, who use their power to organize relations among states. According to this view, it is the rising hegemonic state or group of states—those whose power position has been ratified by war—that defines the terms of the postwar settlement and the character of the new order.[8]

The realist perspective, however, is an inadequate guide to the politics of postwar settlements and the logic of order formation. Settlements are not simply about securing the balance of power or establishing a hegemonic order, even though power matters enormously and victorious states do try to get their way. The distribution of power constrains postwar settlement possibilities, but it does not ultimately determine what is attempted and what is achieved. Order formation is as much a process of solving problems as it is a process of exercising power. Order comes not just from power but from mutual agreement over the conditions of order—over its norms and principles and even over its character as an expression of fairness or justice. At the very least, there are systemic incentives for the leading states to seek such an order. Such incentives stem not from idealist visions or ideological flights of fancy (although particular statesmen have been so motivated) but from the practical realities of putting relations between states back together and doing so with at least a minimal level of legitimacy or mutual agreement.

The most overwhelming issue that confronts state leaders in the aftermath of a major upheaval in the system is the unprecedented uncertainty that prevails—uncertainty about the distribution of power, state interests, and the future relations among the leading states. The basic rules and institutions of diplomacy, security, and economic relations have broken down, and the distribution of power among states has undergone rapid change. States' interests are also more uncertain than they were when the basic character of the international system was relatively stable and known.

The uncertainty that attends postwar junctures has been noted by both participants and observers. Harold Nicolson, who was a British delegate at the 1919 Paris Peace Conference, described his diplomatic history of the settlement as a "study in fog."[9] Confusion and uncertainty reigned as events unfolded and the direction of change remained unclear. Several decades later, U.S. Secretary of State Dean Acheson witnessed the emerging post-

1945 order, and he also found the flow of events confusing. "Not only was the future clouded, a common enough situation, but the present was equally clouded. . . . The significance of events was shrouded in ambiguity. We groped after interpretations of them, sometimes reversed lines of action based on earlier views, and hesitated long before grasping what now seems obvious."[10] Uncertainty is chronic in international relations, but it is particularly acute after major upheavals in the system.

Uncertainty over the postwar environment, coupled with the functional imperatives of rebuilding the basic organization of state relations, infuses the settlement process with a distinctive complexity. As a result, the process of settlement becomes as much one of solving problems as it is one of exercising power.

Three Problems of Order Building

The distinctive politics and logic of order formation can be seen in the problems that wartime and postwar leaders confront. Three are particularly noteworthy: (1) rediscovering and redefining state interests as they relate to systemic order, (2) reassembling and resecuring domestic political coalitions to support state leaders and policy, and (3) securing some minimal level of legitimacy—mutual consent—over the new rules and institutions of postwar order.

The interests of states are less clear to leaders at postwar junctures because the external environment is in flux. It is not clear what type of order will emerge, and it is not clear what goals other states will seek to achieve from the settlement. Although shifts in a state's external environment can occur incrementally and states can initiate a rethinking of basic policy orientations at any time, the incentive, indeed the necessity, to do so dramatically increases at historic breakpoints such as the aftermath of major war. Moreover, the reappraisal of policy is likely to be more basic at these moments. The shifts in the international system and the breakdown in rules and institutions make a basic rethinking of policy unavoidable.

The character of the political debates within leading states and their policy-making processes reflect these changed incentives and possibilities. Popular, scholarly, and governmental writings and studies of a basic foreign policy orientation proliferate at these historical moments. During World War I, the shape of the postwar peace settlement was a subject of debate among British and American peace organizations, political parties, and intellectuals.[11] During World War II, public debate intensified once again, and figures such as Friedrich A. von Hayek, Karl Polanyi, E. H. Carr, and Clarence Streit articulated visions of postwar political and economic order. In the United States, the Council on Foreign Relations was a venue for major policy studies, foreshadowing similar work that was subsequently carried out within the American and British governments.[12] All this activity points to the expanded and basic quality of debate over the proper definition of state interests at critical historical turning points.

Moreover, although state leaders are always concerned with securing or increasing their standing, the problems of maintaining political support intensify during and after a major war. These problems also have a profound impact on the politics of building a postwar settlement. This is true for several reasons. First, war itself mobilizes and activates large parts of the political system. Political leaders put unusual burdens on the society and economy during these periods, and this strains their own political standing. In addition, a major war tends to accelerate the process of change in the underlying structure of relations between the state and society.[13] In the early nineteenth century, the nature of political authority and citizenship changed substantially. In the twentieth century, during and after both wars, change focused on the role of the state in the economy and society, especially in Britain and the United States, where the two world wars brought the character of market society and the social welfare state into particularly sharp focus.[14]

The third problem that state leaders face is building an order that will last, which means that they have an incentive to create an order that is deemed legitimate by the other major states. The sociologist Max Weber argued that all holders of power will seek to legitimate their rule by organizing power relations in a way that will secure the acquiescence of the ruled. "Experience shows that in no instance does domination voluntarily limit itself to the appeal to material or affectual or ideal motives as a basis for its continuance. In addition every such system attempts to establish and to cultivate the belief in its legitimacy."[15] There is a seemingly universal need for those who wield power to exercise that power as legitimate domination.

This incentive to build legitimate power extends into international relations and postwar settlements.[16] Those states that have power after a war have incentives to create order in a way that gains at least a minimal level of assent or acquiescence by others within the system. Rulers enjoy legitimacy when the values that they espouse correspond with the values of those they rule. "If binding decisions are legitimate," Jurgen Habermas, the German social theorist, argued, "that is, if they can be made independently of the concrete exercise of force and of the manifest threat of sanctions, and can be regularly implemented even against the interests of those affected, they must be considered as the fulfillment of recognized norms."[17] When the major states or their leaders share a belief in the normative virtues of a system of order, that system has achieved a measure of legitimacy.

Normative agreement among members is not a necessary condition for the establishment of a stable political order, either domestic or international. Order could be established purely on the basis of coercion, with the hegemonic state using its material resources to induce other states to participate on its terms. Alternatively, order could spring naturally from the free "contracting" actions of states, without any explicit shared norms about order. In the first case, order is based purely on coercive power; in the second case, it is based on a radical convergence of state interests.[18] The history of postwar settlements does not suggest that either of these alternatives is plausible. In each case, war left one or several states in a commanding power position, and there was little initial consensus among the wider array of states on the desired shape of the postwar order. Multiple postwar orders were possible in each instance. Yet, even in these circumstances, powerful states have a strong incentive to build order with some minimal degree of legitimacy and mutual consent, even if they are interested only in advancing their own narrow and short-term interests. A legitimate order is "cost-effective" in that the dominant state will not need to apply coercive power at every turn to maintain control of the system. Whether, and how, shared normative views of a desirable order take shape are additional questions.

Historical Successes and Failures

The environment that postwar leaders face creates problems and incentives that shape the process of order creation. To begin with, it creates incentives for states to debate and, if possible, agree on a set of norms and principles that can guide the overall organization of the postwar system. Because the breakdown of order is widespread, there are functional incentives to agree to an overarching set of terms. One might think of this set as "software" that can be used to run a variety of specific programs. After major breaks in the international system, there are incentives to use this software to tackle the many specific territorial, economic, and political controversies. The embrace of common norms and principles is also a sign of the postwar order's legitimacy, which for separate reasons tends to be a goal of at least the most powerful states.

Second, considerations of legitimacy influence the manner in which defeated states are reintegrated into the postwar system. Even the most powerful states have incentives to rehabilitate defeated states so as to avoid costly and difficult coercive forms of order and control. The incentive to build a "generous peace" is not absolute. It can be overshadowed by other, more immediate and narrow security calculations, but it remains a powerful background incentive.

Finally, states have incentives to find a fit between the newly emerging international order and the domestic challenges facing the major states. The war-induced mobilization and sacrifice of domestic societies and economies and the political instabilities of governing coalitions intensify the relationship between domestic political conditions and the postwar agenda.

These incentives were evident in the Vienna settlement of 1815.[19] The systematic effort to develop a settlement that would be considered legitimate by all sides was manifested in the steps taken to reintegrate France into the European system. Just as important, the character of the treaty itself reflected the complex links between domestic political conditions in the leading states and the interstate settlement. As historians have often noted, the statesmen of 1815 were as concerned with reinforcing their domestic position as they were with reestablishing the balance of power on the Continent.

The importance of legitimacy was manifested most strikingly in the efforts of European state leaders to rehabilitate France by bringing the restored French monarchy back into the Great Power fold. The French government was not required to pay an indemnity, it retained the territories it had held in 1789, and it was eventually accorded full diplomatic status in European politics. Indeed, a hallmark of the Vienna settlement is how successful the European states were in "assimilating" defeated France into the postwar order.[20]

The assimilation process was part of the larger task of building a legitimate order embraced by Castlereagh, Metternich, and Alexander I. The notion of legitimacy was at the heart of the settlement. As former U.S. Secretary of State Henry Kissinger argued in his study of the Congress of Vienna, *legitimacy* refers to "an international agreement about the nature of workable arrangements and about the permissible aims and methods of foreign policy. It implies acceptance of the framework of international order by all major powers, at least to the extent that no state is so dissatisfied that, like Germany after the Treaty of Versailles, it expresses its dissatisfaction in a revolutionary foreign policy."[21]

Legitimacy itself became a norm of postwar order, but legitimacy was more than simply the mutual acceptance of a managed European balance of power. The nature of the states that made up the order was at least as crucial. Although Talleyrand's diplomatic skills were important in negotiating the return of France to Great Power status, the success of the reintegration of France was directly linked to the restoration of the Bourbon monarchy. To the other European leaders, the restoration of the monarchy gave France renewed legitimacy, "the receipt of immediate status and respect from the major European powers and an indication of confidence that other states with 'legitimate' forms of government were willing to accept France on the same diplomatic terms as they had prior to the Revolution."[22] European leaders were as interested in preventing the reoccurrence of the French Revolution and the Napoleonic experience as they were in managing international conflict.[23]

The states whose leaders contemplated order after the Napoleonic wars were themselves in the midst of protracted struggles to define the terms of domestic authority. Although they were governed by ancien régime elites, their societies were modernizing.[24] Therefore, the negotiators sought to establish an order that would contain the upsurge of commercial and democratic society.

By contrast, the settlement of 1919 failed to establish a legitimate postwar order, despite broad discussions of postwar norms and principles stimulated by Wilson's persistent efforts to promote his celebrated Fourteen Points as the basis for a "new diplomacy." Wilson did influence European public opinion and aspects of the final settlement, but the unwillingness of the British and the French governments to acquiesce to several of Wilson's requests—that war reparations be kept to a minimum, that Germany not be occupied, that general disarmament be pursued, and that minorities be granted self-determination—reveals the basic nature of European resistance to Wilson's normative design.[25]

French Premier Georges Clemenceau and British Prime Minister David Lloyd George had very different objectives in securing a postwar settlement. Clemenceau wanted to destroy German power—that is, to establish peace through a preponderance of power. The lessons of the Franco-Prussian War were more relevant to French thinking than was the earlier logic of the Vienna settlement. By contrast, Lloyd George wanted to return to the seeming stability of the nineteenth-century balance-of-power system and British imperial security. Although he was attracted to Wilson's arms control ideas, his vision was one of a return to the old diplomacy rather than one of a bold step into the future. As political scientist Kalevi J. Holsti has argued, "The peacemakers came to Paris with fundamentally different perspectives about the nature of international politics, significantly diverging diagnoses of the causes of the Great War, and largely incompatible recipes for constructing an enduring peace. Each had his own agenda, theories, priorities, visions, and prescriptions."[26]

The result of this discord is well known. Shared norms and principles about power balances and security structures remained elusive, and Germany was not reintegrated into the postwar order. In contrast with the Vienna settlement, the 1919 settlement did not allow representatives of the defeated state to participate in the peace negotiations. Instead, the German representatives were simply handed the terms of peace at the end of the process, a punitive peace that upset many of the American and British officials who participated in the proceedings.

The instability of this outcome was exacerbated by the failure of the negotiators to arrive at a postwar economic settlement. The demand for reparations destroyed the viability of the postwar economic order.[27] The principal problem was the lack of any set of shared economic ideas that could be put on the table for negotiation. The United States, Britain, and France were in the process of evolving away from nineteenth-century laissez-faire economies, but no consensus of views on the meaning of this shift was fully articulated.[28] In the monetary area, for example, the views among experts and politicians about the proper nature of international exchange rate and financial stability varied widely. Therefore, an agreement on basic norms and principles in the economic area was perhaps beyond the grasp of the negotiators, who, in any case, failed even to attempt to reach one.

The 1945 settlement was more successful. In assessing this success, we should recognize that there were, in fact, two settlements after World War II—the settlement between East and West, and the settlement within the West. The settlement among the industrial democratic states is often seen as secondary to and even a by-product of the cold war stalemate. In this view, the West developed cooperative relations primarily in the guise of a security alliance that was held together by the threat from the Soviet Union. The flaw in this analysis is that the logic of relations within the West was settled before the cold war began and largely outside of its shadow. The settlement took the form of a set of liberal multilateral institutions and arrangements, the real and symbolic core of which were the Bretton Woods agreements of 1944.

Several aspects of the 1945 settlement are worth mentioning. First, as in 1919, the United States in 1945 articulated a set of norms and principles of postwar order. There were explicit debates and agreements about the normative foundation of relations among the industrial democracies. Second, the United States was unable simply to use its overwhelming power to induce other states to buy into the American proposals. As the process unfolded, the United States was forced by European resistance and the realities of postwar disarray to modify, dilute, and delay its proposals.[29] In other words, the United States appeared to attempt changes and compromises so as to achieve normative agreement, thereby achieving legitimacy in the postwar order. Third, in specific areas such as postwar monetary and financial rules and institutions, the role of expert consensus between British and American officials was critical to providing a basis for agreement.[30] Uncertainty concerning state interests and the multiple postwar possibilities created opportunities for experts to help shape government conceptions of state interests, particularly in the United States and Britain.

The internal characteristics of the European states in 1945 were more conducive to shifts in the overall normative orientation than they had been in 1919. Initially, support for liberal multilateralism was not widespread in Britain and France. Therefore, American efforts to increase such support involved the use of its material power resources, such as its loan to Britain in 1945–46. This effort was not immediately successful, largely because of the weakness of the British economy. The United States was ultimately able to shape postwar European reconstruction along liberal, regional, and multilateral lines through the Marshall Plan.[31] However, the process by which European officials embraced liberal multilateralism was gradual and was supported by a massive flow of American money and resources.

These ideas were consonant with those of the American New Deal, which emphasized active government and the management of markets and pioneered a domestic vision of organized capitalism in the service of social security, full employment, and growth-oriented public policy. It was a "politics of productivity," in which class differences were submerged by rising incomes, business-labor reciprocity, and social protection.[32] In its international guise, this New Deal synthesis took the form of a managed openness, in which national social protection mechanisms were recognized and secured in a multilateral framework. The establishment of the new postwar economic system, the outline of which was sketched in the 1944 Bretton Woods agreements, was facilitated by the fact that its guiding principles emerged from and resonated with similar sorts of ideas within the leading states, particularly the United States.

Although the Soviet threat had a unifying effect on the Western states, an effect that was important in ensuring the success of the 1945 settlement, the cold war stalemate itself is not a sufficient explanation for this success. The economic settlement also met the demands of the postwar monetary and trade systems, on the one hand, and the evolving requirements of the modern welfare state, on the other. Significantly, the states involved in the settlement of 1945 had comparable capitalist and democratic systems; these similarities increased the chances that they would embrace similar sorts of ordering norms and principles. In this sense, the fateful step after World War II was not so much that the victorious states pursued a "generous peace" but that, led by the United States, they were prepared to intervene in the domestic affairs of the defeated states to reorient the political and economic institutions of those states. The peace was "generous," to be sure, but more important, it was profoundly integrative.

Lessons and Conclusions

The dramatic events of 1991 are unique in history because an international order has been overturned by peaceful change rather than by the horrible violence of continental or global war. The magnitude of change may be as great today as in 1815, 1919, or 1945, but its unfolding has been as unusual as it has been unexpected. Therefore, the differences are as important to acknowledge as the similarities.

The most important difference between the 1990s and the earlier postwar moments is the "peaceful" nature of the breakdown of the old order today. For this we can be grateful. But this reality also denies leaders and diplomats a settlement process in which decisions and agreements can be forged. There will be no formal peace conference this time around. The old order is slipping into history, and the world is not being given the opportunity for a new "constitutional" convention. Problems can be ignored, agreements can be ad hoc, and the principles and norms of order can be left uncertain. The nature of the historical opening that leaders confront may be as important in determining events as the ideas they have in their heads. At earlier postwar junctures, opportunities to shape world order fell into the laps of Western leaders. Today, those opportunities have to be created.

Nevertheless, there is an important similarity between the order building of today and that of the earlier settlements: the "defeated" states must be reintegrated into the system. Here the lesson of 1919 is particularly acute. After 1919 American banks and financial institutions were eager to finance German reconstruction and speed the economic reintegration of Germany into the Western system. But public and congressional opinion remained isolationist and protectionist, and the trade necessary to sustain borrowing remained unrealized. Today the challenge takes the form of whether and how to open Western markets to Eastern Europe and the former Soviet Union. Investment in Eastern Europe again depends on trade flows between Europe and the United States. If the earlier postwar settlements are used as a guide, the fate of the new order will turn on the thorny issue of the reintegration of the defeated states.

Notes

[1]Gordon Craig and Alexander George, *Force and Statecraft* (New York: Oxford, 1983), 31. See also Richard A. Falk, Robert C. Johansen, and Samuel S. Kim, *The Constitutional Foundations of World Peace* (Albany: State University of New York Press, 1993).

[2]Peter J. Katzenstein, "International Relations Theory and the Analysis of Change," in Ernst-Otto Czempiel and James N. Rosenau, eds., *Global Changes and Theoretical Challenges* (Lexington, Mass.: Lexington Books, 1989), 296.

[3]There were, of course, other major wars that produced important settlements in the nineteenth and twentieth centuries. But none of the other European and non-European wars was as large-scale or as destructive (measured, for example, in battle deaths) as these, and none produced treaties or accords that were as sweeping in their postwar designs. See Charles Tilly's discussion of the "ends of wars" in *Coercion, Capital, and European States: AD 990–1990* (Cambridge, Mass.: Basil Blackwell, 1990), 165–70.

[4]Robert Gilpin, *War and Change in World Politics* (New York: Cambridge University Press, 1981), 41–44.

[5]Redvers Opie et al., *The Search for Peace Settlements* (Washington, D.C.: Brookings Institution, 1951), 2–3.

[6]On this general phenomenon, see Charles F. Doran, *The Politics of Assimilation: Hegemony and Its Aftermath* (Baltimore: Johns Hopkins University Press, 1971).

[7]The basic statement of this view is in Kenneth Waltz, *Theory of International Politics* (New York: Wiley, 1979). See also Edward Vose Gulick, *Europe's Classical Balance of Power* (New York: Norton, 1967).

[8]See Gilpin, *War and Change.*

[9]Harold Nicolson, *Peacemaking, 1919* (New York: Grosset and Dunlop, 1965), 6.

[10]Dean Acheson, *Present at the Creation: My Years in the State Department* (New York: Norton, 1969), 3–4.

[11]On the ideas and activities of peace groups during World War I, see Thomas J. Knock, *To End All Wars: Woodrow Wilson and the Quest for a New World Order* (New York: Oxford University Press, 1992), chap. 3.

[12]G. John Ikenberry, "A World Economy Restored: The Anglo-American Postwar Settlement," *International Organization* 46, no. 1 (Winter 1991–92): 289–321.

[13]On the general logic of war, society, and state building, see Tilly, *Coercion, Capital, and European States.* Also see Michael Mann, *States, War, and Capitalism: Studies in Political Sociology* (Oxford: Basil Blackwell, 1988).

[14]See T. H. Marshall, *Sociology at the Crossroads and Other Essays* (London: Heinemann, 1963).

[15]Max Weber, *Economy and Society: An Outline of Interpretive Sociology*, 2 vols., ed. Guenther Roth and Claus Wittich (Berkeley: University of California Press, 1978), 1:213.

[16]Discussions of legitimacy in international politics can be found in various places. See J. W. Burton, *Systems, States, Diplomacy, and Rules* (Cambridge: Cambridge University Press, 1968), chap. 3. The notion of Great Power legitimacy is at the center of Henry Kissinger's study of the Congress of Vienna. See Kissinger,

A World Restored: Metternich, Castlereagh, and the Problems of Peace, 1812–1822 (Boston: Houghton Mifflin, 1957). A discussion of legitimacy as it relates to international law and institutions is found in Thomas M. Franck, *The Power of Legitimacy among Nations* (New York: Oxford University Press, 1990).

[17]Jurgen Habermas, *Legitimation Crisis* (Boston: Beacon Press, 1975), 101.

[18]In this second case, there is a primitive, shared set of understandings about what constitutes the members and rules of the system. As with simple market exchanges, scholars hold a variety of views about whether and how these rational exchange relations are "embedded" in a larger shared normative order.

[19]For a summary of the settlement, see Kalevi J. Holsti, *Peace and War: Armed Conflict and International Order, 1648–1989* (New York: Cambridge University Press, 1991).

[20]See Doran, *The Politics of Assimilation.*

[21]Kissinger, *A World Restored*, 1.

[22]Doran, *The Politics of Assimilation*, 185.

[23]Holsti, *Peace and War*, 115–17.

[24]Frederick B. Artz, *Reaction and Revolution, 1814–1832* (New York: Harper and Row, 1934), chap. 1.

[25]See Knock, *To End All Wars.*

[26]Holsti, *Peace and War*, 178.

[27]This, of course, has been noted in many places, including in the famous statement by John Maynard Keynes, *The Economic Consequences of the Peace* (New York: Harcourt Brace, 1920).

[28]For a statement of the problem that the peacemakers failed to discover a new economic synthesis for the postwar period, see Richard Hofstadter, *The American Political Tradition and the Men Who Made It* (New York: Alfred A. Knopf, 1948), 272–75.

[29]The sequence of American proposals and compromises is outlined in G. John Ikenberry, "Rethinking the Origins of American Hegemony," *Political Science Quarterly* 104 (Fall 1989): 375–400.

[30]This argument is made in Ikenberry, "A World Economy Restored."

[31]Robin Edmonds, *Setting the Mould: The United States and Britain, 1945–1950* (New York: Norton, 1986), chap. 8.

[32]See Charles Maier, "The Politics of Productivity: Foundations of American Economic Policy after World War II," in Peter J. Katzenstein, ed., *The Politics of Productivity: Foreign Economic Policies of Advanced Industrial States* (Madison: University of Wisconsin Press, 1978), 23–49.

Chapter 2

Public Opinion

Ernest R. May

History often affects thinking without one's noticing. That was so in the European upheavals of 1989–91. Especially in Poland and in the Czech and Slovak lands, liberated people looked to the West for sustained interest and support.

This was not because of recent experience, which had been uniformly unencouraging. Despite rhetoric about "rollback," Western governments had stood by, like paralytics, in the 1950s and 1960s while East Berliners, Poles, Hungarians, and Czechs tried to shake off the Soviet yoke. After 1972 Westerners muted even their rhetoric, applauding détente and by implication a permanent Iron Curtain. Journalists and intellectuals joined officials in urging, in effect, that Europeans in the Soviet sphere make the best of their lot. With uncharacteristic acerbity, the future president of Czechoslovakia Václav Havel in 1986 denounced this "naïve, thickheaded, and suicidal way of 'easing tensions.'"[1]

Hope of Western sympathy and help probably flared after 1989 in large part because of memories of Western attitudes and actions *before* the cold war. These were partly memories of the years just after World War II, partly memories of World War I and the Paris Peace Conference. Recalling what America had done after World War II for countries that had recently been its enemies, leaders in the newly freed European republics seemed in 1989–90 to expect a new Marshall Plan. In Washington, Poland's Lech Wałęsa called for "an investment in freedom, democracy, and peace, an investment adequate to the greatness of the American nation."[2] Havel, as the new president of Czechoslovakia, seemed so sure of support for his own country that when he spoke in Washington, it was primarily of the importance of the West's also aiding the still-Communist Soviet Union.

Memories of World War I and its postwar period may have been an even more important nourisher of hope. Every leader in Central and Eastern Europe recalled how Americans and others in the West had aided in shaping and even in creating their nations. Wałęsa often referred to the long history of Western support for Polish independence. On occasion Poles made specific comparisons between the warmth of welcome for Wałęsa and the welcome, during and after World War I, for Ignacy Jan Paderewski. Havel made similar references to the distant past and the strength of sympathy shown for his predecessor, Tomáš Garrigue Masaryk.

Central and Eastern Europeans would be disappointed. President George Bush returned Havel's visit, bringing with him a replica of the Liberty Bell. That came near to being the major tangible proof of Bush's promise to Havel that America would "be part of your nation's democratic rebirth." He declined any debt relief, and his negotiators set hard terms even for trade and investment. West European nations were a little more forthcoming. They rescheduled some debts and in 1991 created a European Bank for Reconstruction and Development with some limited lending capacity. Nevertheless, a comparatively straightforward report in an economic journal in early 1992 was entitled "Paltry Aid to Central Europe." Using softer language, the financier-philanthropist George Soros complained that the Western response had "consistently lagged behind needs of the moment."[3]

Given their recollections of the Marshall Plan and Paris Peace Conference eras and given those ovations for Wałęsa and Havel, Central and East Europeans must have found it especially puzzling that the inaction of Western governments aroused little public criticism. Although Western public opinion could at moments seem ecstatic, it seemed more often to be indifferent or inattentive.

This essay concerns Western public response to the European revolutions of approximately 1919 and approximately 1991. It addresses the question of why that response seemed lively in the earlier period but less so in the more recent one. The answer is, in brief, that Western officials were dubious about making commitments to the new republics both in 1919 and in 1991. In 1919 these officials were overridden. In 1991 they prevailed.

In 1919 officials encountered opposition. Exiles and extra-governmental experts argued that Western governments should support the ideal of national self-determination. These exiles and experts had active support from the press. Sensitive to the press, politicians took positions somewhat at odds with those of officials of their governments. In 1991 nothing similar occurred. No comparable group of exiles existed. Experts outside officialdom had negligible influence. The news media, although incomparably better equipped for reporting events, had lost influence. Subject to little offsetting pressure, politicians in 1991 did pretty much as their government officials bade.

One should note at once that 1919 and 1991 are so different in most respects as to defy comparison, even in these limited terms. The position of the United States relative to Europe had been transformed over the years. The United States itself had changed. In 1919 the American government had scarcely any officials in a British or a European sense. Almost all key posts belonged to politicians or political appointees. Between the two dates, the news media had also changed. And circumstances were totally different. In 1919 Western governments *had* to define the new Europe. In 1991 they could take their time. The ruin caused by World War I and that caused by the cold war had little in common. The recent period owns nothing that can be likened to the Bolsheviks of 1919.

Such differences are important, however, only if historical experiences are being compared as if they provide data for some quasi-mathematical model. If a historical analogy is conceived more as a form of literary metaphor, comparisons can be instructive precisely because they are few and because they are suggestive rather than precise. Setting the Central and East European revolutions of 1919 and 1991 side by side and looking at public responses in the West thus has something in common with exploring, say, the proposition that, in the 1980s, Denis Thatcher was Britain's first lady.

As noted earlier, one similarity is the coolness of Western officialdom. Of course, not *all* officials were cool toward self-determination and democracy, either in 1919 or in 1991. For example, during most of World War I, Sir Ralph Paget and Sir William (later Lord) Tyrell of the British Foreign Office advocated a peace settlement based on the principle of nationality. They called for Polish independence when czarist Russia was still Britain's ally. In the early 1990s, some officers in the U.S. State Department argued for deeper Western commitment to genuine liberation in Europe. Evidence of this came to light in 1993 when three career officers resigned in protest against the West's failure to defend human rights in the remnants of Yugoslavia.[4]

Generally, however, officials in Whitehall and elsewhere were skeptical in 1919 about commitments to either national self-determination or democracy. It would be better, thought most British officials, if national identities found expression within large multinational states. At the Quai d'Orsay, there was stronger support for allowing new nations to come into being. In the French documents that have so far come to light, however, the underlying logic rested wholly on considerations of power. French officials wanted strong states on the other side of Germany, and they were more interested in strength than in ethnic composition. They did worry a bit about Romania's taking in a large Hungarian population, but that was due less to sympathy for Hungarian nationalism than to lack of faith in Romania's reliability as an ally.[5] In 1991 the U.S. State Department and West European foreign ministries were similarly disinclined to risk either money or life for the nations or peoples of Central or Eastern Europe.[6]

Support for Self-Determination

A striking difference between the two periods is the strength in 1919 of apparent public support for policies less cautious and more idealistic than those preferred by officials. During World War I, Western political leaders heard demands to make self-determination for nationalities in Central and Eastern Europe an objective taking precedence over a postwar balance of power. In the more recent period, Western political leaders have heard few cries within their own countries for more active and potentially expensive efforts to aid the newly liberated nations of that region.

In 1919 and thereabouts, some of the clamor came from native Poles, Czechs, and other Central and East Europeans temporarily residing in the West. Among Poles the most prominent were Paderewski and Roman Dmowski. The former spent much of his time in the United States but came to Europe in the period of the Paris Peace Conference. His fame as a pianist gave him entrée almost everywhere. (In Paris he encountered the French premier Georges Clemenceau, who reportedly said to him, "It is really you, Paderewski, the great musician . . . ? And to say that now you are only the prime minister of the Polish republic. What a come down!"[7]) Dmowski had traveled widely before the war. He had, for example, been in the Far East at the time of the Russo-Japanese War and had there become acquainted with a number of Westerners who later became prominent.[8] But Paderewski and Dmowski had assistance from legions of other Poles in exile.

Among Czechs the key figures were Masaryk, Eduard Beneš, and Milan Štefánik. An eminent essayist and philosopher, Masaryk had been one of several leaders of the movement in Bohemia for autonomy within the Austro-Hungarian Monarchy. After the war began, he became an exile when he was warned that the Austrians were planning his arrest. He took up residence in Paris, then moved to London, leaving Beneš and Štefánik behind. The former was effectively Masaryk's alter ego, whereas Štefánik, as the son of a Slovak Lutheran pastor and a distinguished astronomer already long resident in the West, certified the unity of Czechs and Slovaks and helped to open doors in Paris salons.[9]

In 1918 Masaryk toured America. There he found many other Czechs. Some were in exile, but a large number were permanent emigrants. Especially in Chicago and other midwestern cities, Czechs had formed strong political organizations. Apart from lending visible support to Masaryk, they helped his cause by forming an active and effective volunteer counterintelligence corps. Members of this corps won credit and visibility by exposing German sabotage plots.[10]

Southern Slav exiles were as active as Poles or Czechs. Early in the war, Ante Trumbić and Frano Supilo formed a Yugoslav Committee. Its seat was initially in Rome, then in Paris and London. The government of Serbia, headed by Nikola Pašić, pressed the Allies for promises to make postwar Serbia the dominant power in Southeastern Europe. By contrast, Trumbić, Supilo, and others in their committee called for a federation within which

Serbs, Croats, and Slovenes could each fulfill their aspirations for self-government. They enlisted support from large numbers of southern Slavs, both exiles and permanent emigrants, not only in Western Europe and the United States but particularly in Latin America.[11]

Together with representatives of less-well-organized nationalities, these Poles, Czechs, and southern Slavs formed a presence within the bodies politic of Western nations. In Paris, London, Washington, Rome, and other capitals, the appointment books of ministers, backbenchers, and newspaper editors recorded innumerable visits and calls from Paderewski, Dmowski, Masaryk, Beneš, Štefánik, Trumbić, Supilo, or their delegates.

These exiles also kept the cause of self-determination in the public eye. They organized demonstrations designed to win space in newspapers and magazines. In the spring of 1918, they collaborated in holding, in Rome, a massive Congress of the Oppressed Nationalities of the Austro-Hungarian Empire. When Masaryk visited the United States, he joined with other exiles in staging a huge meeting at Carnegie Hall. This was followed a few days later by a public meeting in Philadelphia. There, at Independence Hall, a museum dedicated to the commemoration of the Declaration of Independence of the American colonies, eleven actual or would-be European nations issued a manifesto calling for "the dissolution of the [Habsburg] Empire and the organization of its freed peoples according to their own will."[12]

The exiles of 1919 both maintained an appearance of unity and followed a single, simple line. In reality, the Polish exiles were deeply divided. Endless negotiations would be required for them to agree on Paderewski and Dmowski as their two delegates to the peace conference. Among the Czechs, as well as the Slovaks and Ruthenians, many had conceptions different from Masaryk's. In Bohemia itself, Karel Kramář had a following equal to Masaryk's. Originally an advocate of an independent Czech state under Russian protection, Kramář continued to question Masaryk's plans for a Czechoslovakia oriented toward the West. The southern Slavs and other nationalities were also divided. But they buried or at least disguised their differences, thus becoming able to speak to public opinion and politicians in the West with a single voice stressing a single theme—national self-determination.

Despite their numbers and zeal and skill, the exiles would probably have made little headway had they not had strong support from supposed Central and Eastern Europe experts who were not of Central or East European nationality (or not obviously so). The most formidable—men whose influence reached far beyond their own country—were the experts in England, particularly Lewis Namier, Robert W. Seton-Watson, and G. M. Trevelyan. Namier, now known chiefly for studies of Britain in the eighteenth century, was then celebrated for his translations from and analyses of the Polish press. No one in interwar Britain equaled him in knowledge of contemporaneous Poland. Seton-Watson had published works on German and Austrian history and had traveled in and written about several parts of the Austro-Hungarian Empire. He had met most of the nationalist leaders there, and he was a learned and vigorous champion of self-determination.[13] Trevelyan was the author of a widely read history of Italy's Giuseppe Garibaldi and was thus a presumed authority on militant nationalism.

Some of the experts on Central and Eastern Europe were journalists. The best placed was Henry Wickham Steed. After serving as correspondent for the *Times* of London in Vienna, Wickham Steed succeeded Valentine Chirol as foreign editor for the newspaper. While in Vienna, he had helped and encouraged Seton-Watson, and he himself wrote book-length studies on some of the nationalities of the dual monarchy.

Through Wickham Steed and other journalists and publicists, the slogan of national self-determination was made to seem a cry from the public. At the time, the popular press passed for being both molder of and voice for public opinion. Owners of large circulation dailies believed that they exercised great influence over their readers. Alfred Charles William Harmsworth, Viscount Northcliffe, proprietor of the *Times* and the *Daily Mail,* once declared publicly, "God made people read so that I could fill their brains with facts, facts, facts—and later tell them whom to love, whom to hate, and what to think."[14] Other such press lords included his brother Harold Sidney Harmsworth, Viscount Rothermere, and William Maxwell Aitken, Baron Beaverbrook, in Britain, Jean Dupuy in France, and William Randolph Hearst in the United States. The conservative observer James Bryce, Viscount Bryce, wrote worriedly in 1922 of the capacity of the press "to manipulate news and report selectively according to the interests of its proprietors."[15]

Under the influence of Wickham Steed, Northcliffe became a partisan of self-determination for Poles, Czechs, and others. He pursued this cause with particular zeal because Prime Minister David Lloyd George had put him in charge of wartime propaganda and he judged self-determination to be a slogan that would promote desertions in the enemies' armies. But Northcliffe was not just being expedient. He accepted Wickham Steed's argument that self-determination was the right objective for Britain and the Allies. The news pages as well as the editorial pages of his papers continually made both this case and the case that this was the view and the will of ordinary people in Britain and other Allied lands.

Immediately after the armistice, Northcliffe established a Paris edition of the *Daily Mail* to inform and influence the peacemakers. Wickham Steed wrote something for it every day. In Northcliffe's view, it was "the most important newspaper in the world," for it provided the morning orientation for the British and American delegations, and it supplied cues for other periodicals published in the French capital.[16]

Other publishers—such as Rothermere, Beaverbrook, and Hearst—followed Northcliffe's lead. In the United States, publishers with dailies in major northeastern cities hardly dared do otherwise, given the vigilance of Polish-American, Bohemian-American, and other such organizations.[17] In Italy, the *Corriere della Sera* and the *Secolo* acted as powerful independent supporters of national self-determination. In part, this was an expression of conscience. In part, it was a reaction against the cold, old-fashioned Machiavellianism of Italy's foreign minister, Sidney Sonnino. In part, it was a reflection of the international character of the press, for the editor of *Corriere della Sera*, Luigi Albertini, was a close friend of Wickham Steed's.[18]

At the time, politicians had few ways of gauging public opinion. Elections, of course, were the ultimate tests. Since elections had been suspended during the war in most Allied states, politicians had little to guide them other than fears of what future elections might show. This was true even in America, where the last presidential election had been held in 1916 and the next would not come until 1920. Polls did not yet exist. Periodicals that purported to summarize public opinion did so by making selections from newspapers or magazines. (*Literary Digest*, *Public Opinion*, and *Review of Reviews* were leaders.)

Politicians and analysts of politics tended therefore to take the press at a valuation similar to that of the press lords. The best evidence of this tendency is a thoughtful book published shortly

after the war by the American writer Walter Lippmann. Entitled
Public Opinion, it is in fact a long essay on the press and argued
that the press performed four separate functions. The first function was *map-making*, giving the public their basic sense of the
world in which they lived. The second was *agenda-setting*—that
is, deciding for the public what was important and not important. Third was *influence on government*. Fourth was *use by government*, either for influence on public opinion or for diplomatic
communication or sometimes for intragovernmental communication. Lippmann harshly criticized the performance of these
functions by the press. But he took it for granted that public
opinion would be largely "organized . . . by the press" and
voiced by the press.[19]

The politicians who decided policy in 1919 heard very strong
dissent from the cautious realism of officials of their governments. Their private inclinations varied. Some had none at all.
Italy's leaders tended to think like their officials. Lloyd George
could probably have gone either way with equal contentment
and certainty. He had once said flatly that Austria-Hungary had
to be restored. Later he said the exact reverse. Clemenceau may
have been happy to part company with the Quai d'Orsay. His
later memoirs become uncharacteristically emotional at the point
of the collapse of czarist Russia, as a result of which the French
"war of national defense was transformed . . . into a war of liberation." He continued, "A peace of justice, a Europe founded
upon right, . . . will not this create a body of forces superior to
anything that could come from a powerfully organized frontier?"[20]

Though U.S. President Woodrow Wilson was commonly credited with being the apostle of self-determination, he moved only
slowly into such a stance. His famous Fourteen Points were un-
equivocal only regarding Poland. To the alarm of Masaryk and
others, Wilson spoke there of autonomy for other nationalities
within a re-formed Austro-Hungarian empire. Only after intensive pressure had been applied by the Czechs and their collab-
orators did Wilson edge into a formal commitment to support
independence for others besides the Poles.[21]

Wilson, Clemenceau, and other Allied leaders may personally
have wanted to back Paderewski, Masaryk, and the others. They
may have believed, as Clemenceau suggests, that self-determination would be more likely to preserve peace than would a new
balance of power. Probably, however, they all would have found

it hard to act on such convictions without the belief that public opinion wanted them to do so and might punish them if they did not. This belief gave them armor against officials arguing for policies based more on the principle of the balance of power and on an inclination to maintain the status quo.

In 1991 politicians had no comparable sense that public opinion differed from official opinion. Many Central and East Europeans resided in the West. They were not, however, temporary exiles. They were émigrés who had put down new roots. The Communist governments had curbed emigration and had generally permitted foreign travel only to men or women of proven loyalty. Havel, for example, was offered a fellowship in the United States but decided against accepting it because it would have entailed a permanent break with Czechoslovakia.

Wałęsa, Havel, and their counterparts could conceivably have compensated for not having established a presence in the West comparable to that established by Paderewski, Masaryk, and others. Radio and television enabled them to be heard and seen far more widely. The jet airplane enabled them to be physically present in many more places. In practice, however, their broadcasts and travels were limited. The opportunity to build contacts in the West came after they had assumed responsibility at home. They were thus in positions less like those of Paderewski or Masaryk and more like those of the Polish nationalist leader who remained in Poland, Józef Piłsudski, or Kramář—that is, dependent on delegates.

Another contrast with 1919 was the absence of coordination among Central and East European leaders. For brief periods, Wałęsa and Havel preserved an appearance of cooperation within their own ranks. Havel's foreign minister, the former journalist Jiří Dienstbier, was once quizzed by foreign reporters about how the new Czech leadership managed to seem so much of one mind. He explained that conducting debates underground tended to concentrate minds.[22] But their appearance of unity, even at home, was short-lived. By 1991 factionalism was open and rampant everywhere, and at no time did the new leaders act in concert. From the moment of liberation, they competed with one another for, among other things, favors from the West.

Nor in 1991 were there experts ready or able to play roles comparable to those of Namier, Seton-Watson, and Trevelyan in 1919. Numerically, of course, there were many more experts. Study of the area covered by the Warsaw Pact had become a large industry during the course of the cold war. While most study concentrated on the Soviet Union, particularly the Russian Soviet Republic, Central and Eastern Europe had received some attention. But expertise had become honeycombed. Universities and research centers had specialists on aspects or periods of Central and East European history. A few political scientists, sociologists, and economists were knowledgeable about particular political movements, ethnic groups, or tendencies. None, however, could address policy issues with a breadth, authoritativeness, and certainty comparable to that of Seton-Watson or Wickham Steed in 1919.

Moreover, by 1991 much of the West's expertise on Central and Eastern Europe was owned by officialdom. In Washington the Departments of State and Defense had in-house experts, including those in the State Department's Bureau of Intelligence and Research and in the Defense Intelligence Agency. The Central Intelligence Agency had its own experts, as did the code-breaking, signal-reading National Security Agency. In smaller compass, other Western governments had counterparts. And these in-house experts had an advantage over experts outside because they had access to classified information denied to complete outsiders.

Decline of the News Media

In-house expertise thus left the news media as the one force potentially able to battle the cautious realism of officialdom. (One has to use the half-Saxon, half-Latin term "news media" because of the advent after 1919 first of radio, then of television.) It might be thought that the news media were fully up to the task. In 1991 they had far greater reach than in 1919. Western nations were served by national newspapers with far larger readerships than those of any newspapers of 1919. Some newspapers and magazines in 1991 had international readerships. The *New York Times*, the *Wall Street Journal*, the *Financial Times*, and *Le Monde* are examples of the former. *Time, Newsweek*, the *Economist*, and *Die Zeit* are examples of the latter. Though radio had suffered as a news source after the arrival of television, the British Broadcasting Company (BBC) World Service reached an enormous listenership. And television news coverage had risen to such a high technical level that it provided most people—presidents and prime ministers included—with their primary firsthand reports on crises. It was mostly through Ted Turner's Cable News Network (CNN) and other television reports that the West followed the toppling of Communist governments in Central and Eastern Europe and events such as the tearing down of the Berlin Wall and the abortive coup of August 1991 against Mikhail Gorbachev.

By 1991, moreover, the news media were credited with great political power. The press and television, it was said, had forced the ending of the Vietnam War and the abdication of U.S. President Richard Nixon. Harold Wilson was thought to have become the British prime minister because of the images he could project on the little screen. He himself blamed the press and television for his being driven out of that office.[23] Surely, one might think, the news media of 1991 could have overborne officialdom even without Paderewskis or Masaryks or Namiers or Seton-Watsons.

In fact, the news media of 1991 probably had *less* capacity than the press of 1919 to guide and mold the opinions of interested citizens. In spite of much soul-searching by journalists and politicians about the news media's "power without responsibility," the news media probably also had *less* influence on politicians and governments. Since both of these assertions are apt to seem surprising, they call for some defense.[24]

One reason the news media of 1991 had less influence over public opinion was that their owners and managers did not devote themselves to that objective. The press lords of 1919 had done so. The fact that their era was over probably found its clearest proof in the career of Axel Springer. [25] After World War II, as the Western powers closed down their occupation regimes in Germany, Springer accumulated a publishing empire. His *Bild-Zeitung*, consciously modeled on the British tabloids, became the most popular daily in Germany. At one point, Springer owned 40 percent of Germany's dailies, 80 percent of Germany's Sunday papers, and a significant proportion of all popular magazines.

Springer tried to shape the minds of the *Bild-Zeitung*'s readers not only with editorials but also with news coverage slanted to stimulate German nationalism and economic conservatism. With Northcliffe's example in mind, he acquired *Die Welt*, a Hamburg daily aspiring to be a national newspaper for Germany's elite. He then tried to use *Die Welt* as Northcliffe had used the *Times*.

Springer, however, encountered resistance. His publishing empire became a target for Germany's militant student movement. Students boycotted *Die Welt*. A reporter for the newspaper tells of returning from a long assignment in Asia. "And not only could you not buy *Die Welt* anywhere on a university campus. You didn't even dare carry a copy."[26] Circulation plummeted. Before long, Springer backed off. While *Die Welt*, the *Bild-Zeitung*, and Springer's other publications kept roughly the same editorial lines, editors now made the news pages not much different from those of competing publications.

The reasons for Springer's failure and for the virtual disappearance of the old-fashioned press barons were largely economic. Newspapers depended on advertising. Sales of newspapers themselves rarely covered costs. In 1970 the *Washington Post* took in $13 million from subscriptions and newsstand sales. It spent $20 million just on newsprint.[27] But advertisers paid on the basis of circulation. If the publisher's political campaigns caused circulation to drop, as happened with *Die Welt*, there were immediate consequences. New press barons such as Rupert Murdoch, Robert Maxwell, and Katharine Graham rarely let their prejudices affect their balance sheets. Though Murdoch did what he could to help conservatives, his guiding motto was "to interest the whole community," thereby selling newspapers. Though Maxwell was actually for a time a Labour member of Parliament, he too interfered with editors only when circulations lagged. And Graham from time to time acquiesced to editorial lines with which she herself did not agree.[28]

Increasingly, professional journalists gained control over the content of newspapers and magazines. Most professional journalists regarded news management à la Northcliffe and his like as unprofessional. By 1991 few editors would tolerate being ordered by publishers to play up certain issues or regions or to bend news for a cause, even if a good one. And few reporters would tolerate being told by editors to slant their stories.

Editors, however, were not unaffected by the economic pressures bearing down on their publishers. This is not to say that editors made news judgments in terms of what would sell or, less still, that they toadied to particular advertisers. But economic realities made it hard for editors to continue giving news space to subjects not manifestly of interest to readers. Northcliffe could keep Central and Eastern Europe on the front pages of the *Times* and the *Daily Mail* week after week because he believed that the public *ought* to be interested. No one responsible for a major daily or weekly had that luxury in 1991.

In an earlier time, foreign news occupied a special niche. Until at least the 1950s, the foreign editors of newspapers, newsmagazines, and even radio networks had reason to suppose that they selected reports for a special, restricted audience. Survey research suggested that the potential "foreign policy public" totaled not much more than 15 percent of the public generally interested in public affairs.[29] When foreign news was given space or airtime, the selection criteria could be somewhat different from those for local or national news. By 1991 this had ceased to be true. Foreign news competed for space or time on an even basis with other news. Its chances of appearing depended on whether it qualified as what a Hearst editor once characterized as "anything that makes a reader say 'Gee whiz!'"[30]

Competition within newspapers and magazines was affected by a trend toward bureaucratization that accompanied the trend toward professionalization. The print news media had become by 1991, in sociologist Herbert J. Gans's phrase, "bureaucracies staffed by professionals."[31] Reporters received specialized beats. Newsrooms became as compartmentalized as beehives. The writer Gay Talese described the *New York Times* when Turner Catledge became managing editor: "Each morning hundreds of people would file into the newsroom and would either seat themselves behind vast rows of desks like parishioners at church, or they would disappear in the distance behind some pillar or interior wall, some dark nook or glass-enclosed maze on the doors of which was printed 'Science' or 'Real Estate' or 'Drama' or 'Sports' or 'Society'—and even when Catledge stood outside his own office gazing around the newsroom through his binoculars he could never see at a single sweep everybody on his staff nor did he precisely know what they were all doing there."[32]

While decisions on reporters' assignments and on the space and placing of stories were based on professional criteria, they also became in some sense corporate decisions. Bargaining went on just as within large business organizations or government agencies. Political scientist Leon V. Sigal described battles at the *New York Times* over whether a presidential speech at the United Nations would belong to the metropolitan staff, the national desk's White House correspondent, or the foreign desk's United Nations correspondent.[33]

Television, of course, had much to do with this change. Television made no distinction between domestic and foreign news, and television had quickly become the public's preferred source of news. Though most evidence on this point came from the United States, the same preference appeared in surveys run in France and in Yugoslavia. And, at least among Americans, the preference for television over print was especially marked regarding international news. In a 1985 survey commissioned by American newspaper editors, the vote in favor of television over newspapers as a source for world news was 72 percent to 18 percent.[34]

Newspapers and magazines competed with television to report hot stories. For all the news media, however, coverage of foreign affairs became increasingly difficult because it was increasingly expensive. Newspapers steadily reduced numbers of foreign bureaus. In 1945 American newspapers had about twenty-five hundred reporters abroad. By 1969 the number was under six hundred, and by the mid-1970s it was well under five hundred. Even the *New York Times* scaled back. It had more than sixty foreign correspondents in the 1950s, but by 1978 there were only thirty-four.[35] Between 1965 and 1976 the *Times* of London reduced its number of foreign correspondents from twenty-six to eighteen; the *Daily Telegraph* cut back from thirty to thirteen.[36]

Newspapers became increasingly reliant on the shallow coverage provided by wire services. Television news obtained much of its foreign footage from Visnews or UPITN, the former a sort of television wire service dominated by the BBC, the latter a partnership between United Press International and British Independent Television News. These services provided pictures without commentary. The only sounds were those of the action on film (as one writer remarked, "the thud of rifle butts on heads, perhaps").[37] Each network or station could supply its own words.

The results of all these changes for the map-making and agenda-setting functions of the news media are suggested by a few figures. Under the heading "Czechoslovakia," the *New York Times* index for 1991 lists 51 stories; that for 1919 lists 118. Of *Times* stories on Czechoslovakia for 1991, 2 appeared on page 1; another 12 were on pages 2 to 4. Of *Times* stories for 1919, 12 were on the front page; 41 others were on pages 2 to 4.[38] Under the same heading, the *Reader's Guide to Periodical Literature* for

1991 listed 18 articles, whereas the heading for 1919 listed 31—despite the fact that the *Reader's Guide* for 1991 indexed almost twice as many magazines (209 as opposed to 112).

Unquestionably, people in the West interested in Czechoslovakia or other parts of Central or Eastern Europe in 1991 could obtain more information than could their counterparts of 1919. When a story from the area did show up on page 1 of the *New York Times* or figured in network television news in 1991, it was better covered than any story of 1919. But in 1991 the news media did not keep the region more or less constantly before the potentially interested public as it had in 1919. News media coverage did little to suggest to Western political leaders that a large public cared about revolutions in the region.

This brings us to the second proposition, namely that the ability of the news media to influence politicians and governments was less in 1991 than it had been in 1919. In part, the explanation for lessened influence is the rise of competition. Politicians no longer looked to newspapers and magazines as the primary indexes of public opinion. Nor did they look to television news. From the 1930s onward, political leaders in the West made increasing use of public opinion polls. The art of polling became more and more sophisticated, and polls became increasingly reliable predictors of market trends and election outcomes. President Jimmy Carter put a pollster on his White House staff. He made almost no major decision without first having a telephone survey conducted or a focus group consulted. Despite Carter's election loss in 1980, the use of polls remained standard practice for his successors and was copied elsewhere.[39]

Instead of fighting this competition, the news media came to treat polls as news—that is, as the facts about public opinion. The *New York Times*, the *Washington Post*, the *Wall Street Journal*, the *Los Angeles Times*, and the major television networks began to commission and publish public opinion polls and to run front-page stories on the results. This shift in itself reflected some surrender of the third function that Lippmann had assigned the news media—that of influencing government by speaking *for* public opinion.

The potential influence of the news media on politicians and policy was also affected by increased intimacy. In 1919 officials and journalists had little to do with one another. In *Public Opinion*, Lippmann quoted a fellow journalist's complaint about press agents: "The great corporations have them, the banks have them, the railroads have them, all the organizations of business and of social and political activity have them. . . . Even statesmen have them."[40] Note the choice of words: *even* statesmen.

When Lippmann wrote, governments had just begun to use press offices. The British Foreign Office created a News and Political Intelligence Department in 1919. Its head was Sir William Tyrell, one of the Foreign Office mandarins. He would be long remembered by British journalists for his frankness regarding the government-press relationship. Tyrell once said to a group of reporters: "You think we lie to you. But we don't lie, really we don't. However, when you discover that, you make an even greater error. You think we tell you the truth."[41]

In the United States, press offices began to take form during the 1930s, mostly to protect or propagandize for controversial New Deal agencies such as the Tennessee Valley Authority. In 1936 a congressional inquiry identified 270 federal public affairs officers, many part-time. In 1977, when Congress counted again, there were 3,366, and this number was for only the twenty largest agencies.[42]

These armies of public affairs officers performed many functions, the number and variety growing over time. In the early 1960s, a scholar studying press-government relations in Washington divided public affairs officers into three categories: informers ("just the facts"), educators (or explainers), and promoters.[43] In that period of "high" cold war, public affairs officers in all three categories acted partly as guardians of the government's secrets and partly, even if trying only to inform or educate, as missionaries. A not untypical attitude was voiced by President Dwight D. Eisenhower's first national security assistant, Robert Cutler: "In this world, where freedom as never before struggles rawly for survival [the news media] must make clear how they will contribute to our survival; they must prove to us that the widespread, public disclosure of our secret projects will make the free world stronger, and the neutrals better disposed; will rally the subject peoples, and will put the Communist regimes at a disadvantage."[44]

Intentness on somehow controlling the news media increased during the 1960s. Robert Manning, who managed press relations for the U.S. State Department in the early 1960s, concluded that most officials had little understanding of the news media and little interest in trying to manage news media relations. In contrast, Philip Goulding, who had a similar post in the Defense Department later in the decade, testified to carefully planned campaigns playing on the prejudices, weaknesses, and strengths of particular correspondents.[45]

A similar shift occurred in the U.S. Congress. A former aide to Senator J. William Fulbright, the chairman of the Foreign Relations Committee, commented that as of 1962–63, Fulbright avoided both interviews with reporters and appearances on television. The situation was different by 1970, said the aide: "There had been quite a change. Advance speech texts and press releases were the rule. The Senator himself was well aware that in order to make the evening news shows it was wise to do the filming around noon—never after 4 p.m.—to permit the networks to plan for it."[46]

Looking at the press-government relationship from the reporters' side, scholars have concluded that the relationship worked increasingly in favor of the government. Several scholars have drawn analogies with markets, characterizing officials as sellers, reporters as buyers. Though officials might be eager to sell their stories for any of many reasons, they have some freedom to choose among buyers. The reporters have less time and less opportunity to shop among sources. Moreover, the reporters are constrained by being in some sense middlemen. Once a reporter has a piece of news, he or she still has to persuade an editor or producer to use it. The more rare the tidbit offered by the official, the higher is its value to the reporter in terms of his or her competition for space. In this picture, the reporter is a buyer in a sellers' market but a seller in a buyers' market.[47]

Not surprisingly, officials became able, to some degree, to determine the terms of trade. They could stipulate that information was provided off the record—that is, with nothing to be published showing that any information had been provided. They could stipulate that it was "background," meaning that the informant would not be identified. The commonness of news stories citing anonymous "sources" led writer Ward Just to write: "Walter and Ann Source had four daughters, 'Highly Placed, Authoritative, Unimpeachable, and Well-Informed.' The first married a diplomat named U.S. Officials and the second a government public relations man named Reliable Informant."[48]

Students of the relationship saw several reasons why reporters would tend to become captives of their sources. The *New York Times*'s Russell Baker observed that reporters became assimilated to their beats: "The State Department reporter quickly learns to talk like a fuddy-duddy and to look grave, important, and inscrutable. The Pentagon man always seems to have just come in off maneuvers."[49] Case studies further suggest that reporters sometimes became integral parts of the organizations they covered. Reporters' discourse tended to be with their sources rather than with their editors or readers or even their fellow reporters.

A substantial body of analysis thus suggests that by 1991 there was more use of the news media by government than the reverse. The use was likely to be cautious and respectful, not manipulative in the popular sense of the term. Few officials forgot that if there was a last word, it would be the reporters', not theirs. In his study of newsmagazines and television networks, Gans describes officials and reporters as similar to dancers, with both parties cooperating and keeping step but with officials giving the lead.[50]

From top to bottom, the news media of 1991 were thus different from the press of 1919. They did not attempt to mold public opinion in the same degree. Rather, they catered to opinion as it existed at any moment. Nor did they undertake in any comparable way to represent themselves as voices of the public. Instead, they reported the results of public opinion polls. And, because of the new intimacy between officials and reporters, what the news media said about the world reflected officials' attitudes rather than, as in 1919, challenging those attitudes.

It should be stressed again that 1919 and 1991 can be compared only metaphorically (as one might compare Hillary Rodham Clinton and Denis Thatcher). The benefit comes from having the eye drawn to some feature of the one or the other that might have gone unremarked. Setting Western public response to the European revolutions of 1989–91 side by side with the response to those of 1917–19 stimulates notice that Western officialdom was cool in both periods. In the earlier period, the cautiousness of officialdom was offset by apparent enthusiasm among the public for the ideal of "national self-determination." In the later period, public opinion seemed either indifferent or disposed, like officialdom, to leave the area to itself.

The apparent public enthusiasm of 1919 was traceable to deliberate stimulation by exiles such as Paderewski and Masaryk, abetted by experts such as Seton-Watson and Wickham Steed. Press lords led by Northcliffe then kept the evidence of enthusiasm before the eyes of politicians, impressing all of them with the possible electoral risks of doing as officials wanted and concentrating on the reconstruction of a balance of power.

The apparent lukewarmness of Western public opinion in 1991 can be explained by the absence of these factors. No comparable exiles existed. There were few experts outside officialdom but many within. There were no press lords. Professionally run news media catered to popular interests instead of creating them. As a result, Western policies reflected the kind of "realism" for which political scientist Hans Morgenthau and diplomat and historian George F. Kennan had pleaded just after World War II and little or none of the "moralism" that they had deplored then, when looking back at World War I.

Was this a good outcome? The answer probably depends on whether the respondent is a Western official or a Pole or a Czech.

Notes

[1] Václav Havel, *Disturbing the Peace: A Conversation with Karel Hvizhdzala* (New York: Alfred A. Knopf, 1990), 122. The original version was *Dálkovy vyslech* (Prague: Rozmluvy, 1986).

[2] *Washington Post*, 29 June 1990, A-2.

[3] Richard E. Feinberg, "Paltry Aid to Central Europe," *Challenge: The Magazine of Economic Affairs* 35 (January-February 1992): 36–43; George Soros, *Underwriting Democracy* (New York: Free Press, 1991), 248.

[4] Harold I. Nelson, *Land and Power: British and Allied Policy on Germany's Frontiers, 1916–1919* (Toronto: University of Toronto Press, 1963), 8–13; see, among others, Laura Blumenfeld, "A Sense of Resignation: The Bosnia Dissenters," *Washington Post*, 28 August 1993.

[5] Nelson, *Land and Power*, 111–19.

[6] See Philip Zelikow and Condoleeza Rice, *Germany Unified and Europe Transformed: A Study in Statecraft* (Cambridge, Mass.: Harvard University Press, 1995).

[7] Jean-Baptiste Duroselle, *Clemenceau* (Paris: Fayard, 1988), 815.

[8] See the memoir by Colonel Edward Mandell House's peace conference aide, Stephen Bonsal, *Suitors and Suppliants: The Little Nations at Versailles* (New York: Prentice-Hall, 1946), chap. 7.

[9] Robert W. Seton-Watson, *A History of the Czechs and Slovaks* (London: Hutchinson, 1943), 287–89.

[10] Tomáš Garrigue Masaryk, *The Making of a State: Memories and Observations, 1914–1918* (New York: Frederick A. Stokes, 1927), 259–62.

[11] See, in general, Ivo J. Lederer, *Yugoslavia at the Paris Peace Conference* (New Haven: Yale University Press, 1963).

[12] Seton-Watson, *Czechs and Slovaks*, 306; Victor S. Mamatey, *The United States*

and East Central Europe, 1914–1918: A Study in Wilsonian Diplomacy and Propaganda (Princeton: Princeton University Press, 1957), 316–17.

[13]The best single book on the shaping of pro-self-determination opinion in 1919 is the Seton-Watson biography written by his two sons, Hugh Seton-Watson and Christopher Seton-Watson, *The Making of a New Europe* (Seattle: University of Washington Press, 1981).

[14]Hugh Cudlipp, *The Prerogative of the Harlot: Press Barons and Power* (London: Bodley Head, 1980), 82.

[15]Quoted in Denis McQuail, *Review of Sociological Writing on the Press*, Royal Commission on the Press Working Paper No. 2 (London: Her Majesty's Stationery Office, 1976), 12.

[16]Henry Wickham Steed, *Through Thirty Years, 1892–1922: A Personal Narrative*, 2 vols. (London: William Heinemann, 1924), 2:260.

[17]See Mamatey, *The United States and East Central Europe*, and Joseph P. O'Grady, ed., *The Immigrants' Influence on Wilson's Peace Policies* (Lexington: University of Kentucky Press, 1967).

[18]See Luigi Albertini, *Venti anni di vita politica*, pt. 2, 3 vols. (Bologna: Nicola Zanichelli, 1953), 3:236–53.

[19]Walter Lippmann, *Public Opinion* (New York: Macmillan, 1922), 32.

[20]Georges Clemenceau, *Grandeur and Misery of Victory* (New York: Harcourt Brace, 1930), 192.

[21]Mamatey, *The United States and East Central Europe*. See also Arthur S. Link, ed., *Woodrow Wilson and a Revolutionary World, 1913–1921* (Chapel Hill: University of North Carolina Press, 1982), especially the essays by Kay Lundgreen-Nielsen and Inga Floto.

[22] Misha Glenny, *The Rebirth of History: Eastern Europe in the Age of Democracy* (London: Penguin Books, 1990), 2.

[23] Michael Cockerell, *Live from Number 10: The Inside Story of Prime Ministers and Television* (London: Faber and Faber, 1988), 87, 104–5, 140–41.

[24] For examples, see James Curran and Jean Seaton, *Power without Responsibility: The Press and Broadcasting in Britain*, 4th ed. (London: Routledge, 1991); Caroline Rees, "The Abuse of Picture Power (The Press)," *New Statesman* 108 (28 September 1984): 8–10; Jean-François Revel, "The Power of 'The Fourth Estate,'" *Encounter* 69, no. 4 (November 1987): 37–42 (on France); and almost any issue of *Nieman Reports*. What follows here borrows heavily from my essay "The News Media," in Gordon Craig and Francis Loewenheim, eds., *The Diplomats, 1939–1979* (Princeton: Princeton University Press, 1994).

[25] Hans Dieter Muller, *Press Power: A Study of Axel Springer* (London: Macdonald and Company, 1969); Martin Walker, *Powers of the Press: Twelve of the World's Influential Newspapers* (New York: Adama Books, 1982), chap. 4.

[26] Friedheim Kremna, quoted in Walker, *Powers of the Press*, 96.

[27] Leon V. Sigal, *Reporters and Officials: The Organization and Politics of Newsmaking* (Lexington, Mass.: D. C. Heath, 1973), 9.

[28] See William Shawcross, *Rupert Murdoch, Ringmaster of the Information Circus* (London: Chatto and Windus, 1992); Joe Haines, *Maxwell* (London: Macdonald,

1988); Deborah Davis, *Katharine the Great: Katharine Graham and Her* Washington Post *Empire*, 3d ed. (New York: Sheridan Square Press, 1991); and Carol Felsenthal, *Power, Privilege, and the* POST: *The Katharine Graham Story* (New York: Putnam's, 1992).

[29] V. O. Key, *Public Opinion and American Democracy* (New York: Alfred A. Knopf, 1961), 173–74; Robert W. Oldendick and Barbara Ann Bardes, "Mass and Elite Foreign Policy Opinions," *Public Opinion Quarterly* 46 (Winter 1982): 368–82.

[30] Sigal, *Reporters and Officials*, 1.

[31] Herbert J. Gans, *Deciding What's News: A Study of CBS Evening News, NBC Nightly News, Newsweek, and Time* (New York: Pantheon Books, 1979), 84. Stephen Hess, *The Washington Reporters* (Washington, D.C.: Brookings Institution, 1981), 42–43, makes the point, however, that newspaper bureaus are less bureaucratic than other organizations of comparable size and complexity, largely because of reporters' horror of bureaucracy. On the bureaucratization of journalism, see— in addition to Gans, Hess, and Sigal, *Reporters and Officials*—Gaye Tuchman, *Making News: A Study in the Construction of Reality* (New York: Free Press, 1978), which is based on extended observations of both newspaper and television newsrooms.

[32] Gay Talese, *The Kingdom and the Power* (New York: World, 1966), 212.

[33] Sigal, *Reporters and Officials*, 21.

[34] Claude Bellanger et al., *Histoire Générale de la Presse Française*, 5 vols. (Paris: Presses Universitaires de France, 1969–76), 5:211; James F. Larson, "Global Television and Foreign Policy," in Foreign Policy Association, *Headline Series* 283 (February 1988): 22–23.

[35] Mort Rosenblum, *Coups and Earthquakes: Reporting the World for America* (New York: Harper and Row, 1979), 9, 29.

[36] Oliver Boyd-Barrett, "The Collection of Foreign News in the National Press," Part A of Royal Commission on the Press, *Studies on the Press* (London: Her Majesty's Stationery Office, 1977), 15–19.

[37] Jeremy Tunstall, *The Media Are American* (New York: Columbia University Press, 1977), 48.

[38] As evidence that this was not a straight-line decline, one should note that the high point of coverage was 1948. The *New York Times Index* for that year has 479 entries under "Czechoslovakia"; 50 of these were front-page stories; 190 appeared on pages 1 through 4.

[39] See Susan Herbst, *Numbered Voices: How Opinion Polling Has Shaped American Politics* (Chicago: University of Chicago Press, 1993).

[40] Lippmann, *Public Opinion*, 344.

[41] Quoted in Sigal, *Reporters and Officials*, 131.

[42] David Morgan, *The Flacks of Washington: Government Information and the Public Agenda* (New York: Greenwood, 1986), 19–25.

[43] Dan D. Nimmo, *Newsgathering in Washington* (New York: Atherton, 1964).

[44] Quoted in Douglass Cater, *The Fourth Branch of Government* (New York: Random House, 1959), 115–16.

[45] Robert Manning, *The Swamp Root Chronicle: Adventures in the Word Trade* (New York: Norton, 1992), 231; Phil G. Goulding, *Confirm or Deny* (New York: Harper and Row, 1970), 220–21.

[46] Walter Pincus, quoted in Sigal, *Reporters and Officials*, 127.

[47] Both Gans, *Deciding What's News*, and Sigal, *Reporters and Officials*, develop the market analogy.

[48] Quoted in Robert J. McCloskey, "The Care and Handling of Leaks," in Simon Serfaty, ed., *The Media and Foreign Policy* (London: Macmillan, 1990), 114.

[49] Quoted in Sigal, *Reporters and Officials*, 48.

[50] Gans, *Deciding What's News*, 34. On the general issue, see Richard V. Ericson, Patricia M. Baranek, and Janet B. L. Chan, *Negotiating Control: A Study of News Sources* (Toronto: University of Toronto Press, 1989).

Chapter 3

Disturbed Spirits: Minority Rights and New World Orders, 1919 and the 1990s

Michael Burns

> ". . . there cannot be any peace with disturbed spirits, there cannot be any peace with a constantly recurring sense of injustice. . . . every race should have justice."
>
> Woodrow Wilson, address to B'nai B'rith,
> December 1918

The Paris Peace Conference of 1919 and the international negotiations of the early 1990s share a backdrop of chaos. In the wake of World War I, debates over the recognition of new states and minority rights, like debates over the same subjects in the aftermath of the cold war, took place in a world marked by massive economic dislocation, inflamed nationalism, and internecine struggle. During both periods—following the collapse of the Habsburg, Hohenzollern, Romanov, and Ottoman Empires and after the fall of the Soviet Union and the fracturing of Yugoslavia—negotiators confronted refugee crises, xenophobic reactions, religious violence, and an array of ethnic conflicts. Arriving in Paris in the spring of 1919, the American progressive Oswald Garrison Villard noted that the number of wars "going on in the world had grown to fourteen . . . one war for each of [Wilson's] peace terms"; and in the summer of 1993, former President Jimmy Carter, attending the Vienna Conference on

Human Rights, counted thirty-two major conflicts in the world, most of them civil wars.[1]

Across the century, from Sarajevo to Sarajevo, movements launched in the name of self-determination have contributed to the shattering of old states and the creating of new nations. The century that opened with barely fifty recognized states ends with nearly two hundred, and there are, at last count, some five thousand distinct peoples in the world, not a few of whom long for autonomy or independence. The history of imperialism and decolonization reveals more about those diverse national sentiments than does the history of the Paris Peace Conference. But the new European order fashioned in 1919 signaled a seismic shift in the definition of self-determination, in the nature of the modern state, and in the plight of minority populations.[2] As social anthropologist Ernest Gellner has said, peacemakers at the 1814–15 Congress of Vienna imposed a system of boundaries that was "stoically indifferent to the ethnic principle." Not until the "Wilsonian stage" did a new generation of peacemakers attempt to implement the nationalist principle that had been gaining legitimacy across the nineteenth century. And when they did—when they redrew the map of Central and Eastern Europe as far as possible along lines of ethnicity, language, and culture—they created a system with "all the weaknesses of the previous empires and a lot of weaknesses of its own."[3] The result, Gellner concluded, was "a catastrophe" that even Woodrow Wilson came to recognize. The president remarked near the close of the conference: "When I gave utterance to those words (that all nations had a right to self-determination), I said them without the knowledge that nationalities existed which are coming to us day after day. . . . You do not know the anxieties that I have experienced as a result of the many millions of people having their hopes raised by what I have said." The secretary of state, for whom Wilson had little respect and even less time, proved to be the most accurate visionary in Paris. The phrase "self-determination" is "simply loaded with dynamite," Robert Lansing warned. "Will it not breed discontent, disorder, and rebellion? . . . What a calamity that the phrase was ever uttered!"[4]

The Great Powers of 1919, like their successors at the end of the century, encouraged centrifugal forces of self-determination and then confronted an aftershock of the new order—the crisis of national minorities. Of the one hundred million people detached from the pre–World War I empires of Central and Eastern Europe, nearly thirty million (almost one-third of the total population of thirteen European states) became "national minorities." According to historian Robert W. Seton-Watson, the inclusion of three million Germans and three-quarters of a million Magyars "placed Czechoslovakia high on the list of countries faced by a minority problem."[5] Poland's minorities included one million Germans, more than three million Jews, and four million Ukrainians, along with tens of thousands of Lithuanians and White Ruthenians. To the south, Croatia, Dalmatia, and parts of Slovenia, as well as the whole of Bosnia and Herzegovina with its large Muslim population, were joined to the kingdom of Serbia, the population of which grew to over twelve million. More than 30 percent of the Hungarian population found themselves outside the historic boundaries of the Carpathian Basin (primarily in Romania, Czechoslovakia, and Yugoslavia), and while Hungary lost nearly 70 percent of its territory (much of it rich in natural resources), the size of Romania more than doubled, as did its population.[6]

Even the most fastidious matchmakers of state and culture realized in 1919 that self-determination could never be "Simon-pure" and that any new boundary would leave national minorities "on one side or the other," often in the midst of resentful populations. Languages and religions were too "closely intermingled," as one contemporary put it, and "no power on earth could disentangle . . . Poles and Ruthenians in Galicia, Magyars and Romanians in Transylvania, Serbs and Romanians in the Banat."[7] The murderous quest for national purity would start in earnest barely two decades later, and it would continue at the end of the century, but the Paris peacemakers believed that national sovereignty could be honored and minorities protected through bilateral treaties and the new mechanism of the League of Nations Covenant and the Permanent Court of International Justice. Today, in the aftermath of 1991, the words of the secretary-general of the United Nations (UN) sound like echoes from the conference halls of Paris. Boutros Boutros-Ghali wrote in August 1993, "Perhaps the post–Cold-War era's most fundamental task [is] the defense and strengthening of a cooperative and healthy international state system while defending legitimate minority rights within state borders."[8]

The following account of minority rights in 1919 and the 1990s charts the ongoing conflict "between nation and world," between national sovereignty and international guarantees.[9] It examines precedents drawn upon and precedents set in Paris, and from the League Covenant to the most recent World Conference on Human Rights, it explores the tension between advocates of particularistic group rights and proponents of the universalist formula of individual rights. With all the discontinuities and differences of historical context, the international negotiations that followed the Great War and the cold war share a timeless reality. "My apologies to the memory of Attila," said Georges Clemenceau, French premier and president of the Paris Peace Conference, "but the art of arranging how men are to live is more complex even than the art of massacring them."[10]

Minority Rights at Paris

Promising a "new departure" from old habits of international relations, Wilson sailed for Paris in December 1918 accompanied by geographers, statisticians, historians, and political scientists who pledged to work like "engineers" on a "new construction project." Submitting blueprints of peace, they believed the "credo [that] international policies functioned in a truly rational universe." One of Wilson's advisers, a member of the Inquiry group, applied that thinking to the Balkans. "Whichever way the problem is handled," he wrote on the eve of the conference, "the scientist may safely conclude that any solution which does not treat the Jugoslavs as one nation is based on unscientific foundations and hence cannot be considered a permanent solution."[11]

The historical record reveals, however, that those top-hatted armies of rational diplomats and academicians did not methodically design a new European order in 1919 as much as scurry to redesign a fait accompli. Through the previous fall and winter, national revolutions had led to the establishment, in "rough and provisional fashion," of new states formed from crumbling empires.[12] Along with Czechoslovakia, Austria, Hungary, and the Serb-Croat-Slovene kingdom came the vastly transformed state of Romania and the approaching reality of Polish independence. Before the conference opened and through the months it convened, boundaries were redrawn on the spot, often by means of armed conflict, and with the chaos came calls for protection. "The hopes of all minority groups in Eastern Europe rest upon the whole-hearted sympathy that you have unfailingly evinced for the oppressed," a leading member of the American Jewish

Congress, Louis Marshall, wrote Wilson in Paris. "It is therefore that I . . . call your attention to the atrocities to which the Jews of Poland and Galicia have recently been subjected." Marshall went on to describe "the murder of Jews in Pinsk, Lida, and Wilna" and reminded Wilson of his recent comments on the protection of Yugoslav peoples. "The family of nations," the president had announced, must "abundantly safeguard the liberty, the development, and all the just rights of national or racial minorities." From his White House secretary, Wilson received a telegram urging that rhetoric give way to action. Describing a mass meeting at Madison Square Garden to protest killings in Poland and elsewhere, the secretary warned: "Feeling in this matter is growing more intense. . . . Cannot something be done?"[13]

Something was done in Paris, though late in the day. The League of Nations Covenant, the first item on the conference agenda, had contained no specific provision on minority rights, nor did the treaty with Germany, which the Supreme Council continued to debate. But in late April, Wilson, Clemenceau, and David Lloyd George (the Italian prime minister, Vittorio Emanuele Orlando, was off on his voyage of protest over Fiume) finally turned from abstract pronouncements to concrete plans. And they did so "at the insistence" of Jewish delegations representing groups based in Britain, the United States, Poland, Romania, Greece, Italy, Holland, and elsewhere. Though the delegates' internal debates were sometimes rancorous (Zionists and Jewish assimilationists fought without resolution, for example, over Palestine and the nature of cultural autonomy within Europe), most agreed on one key point: they would petition for the equal treatment of all "confessions, races, and languages" in the new European states.[14] In its specific origins, if not in its broad outlines, the minorities question in Paris was a Jewish question.

The Polish treaty, largely drafted by British and American Jews working with the Committee on New States, emerged as the model agreement.[15] Revised clauses would apply to individual states (references to Jews in the Polish and Romanian documents would be replaced by references to Muslims in the treaties with Greece and Yugoslavia and to Ruthenians in the treaty with Czechoslovakia), but they shared common guarantees. Along with civil and religious equality, national minorities would have the right to use their own language in private relations and in the courts; they would receive state and communal funds for educational, religious, and welfare purposes; and they would have the right to primary education in their own language. However, this would not prevent the state from requiring the teaching of the national language in all schools, and special provisions in the Polish treaty allowing Jews to observe the Sabbath without penalty would not exempt them from military service.[16]

The minorities treaties confirmed that the Great Powers straddled the diplomacy of two centuries. Formal recognition of the cultural rights of "national minorities" set a crucial precedent, whereas the language of the treaties echoed earlier agreements. Documents drafted at the Congress of Vienna in 1814–15 had included limited guarantees of religious and legal equality for minority populations, and in 1830 the protocol recognizing the Kingdom of Greece as the first state formed from the Ottoman Empire had demanded that all subjects of the new states be "treated on the footing of perfect equality, without regard to difference of creed in their relations, religious, civil, or political." The 1878 Congress of Berlin, the precedent most often cited in Paris, had placed strict conditions on the recognition of Serbian and Romanian independence: "The difference of religious creeds and confessions shall not be alleged against any person as a ground for exclusion or incapacity in matters relating to the enjoyment of civil and political rights." Indeed, Romania's flagrant violations of the 1878 agreement, especially regarding its Jewish subjects, helped prepare the explicit safeguards of 1919.[17]

But another nineteenth-century precedent drew fire from the leaders of new Central and East European states. As in the past, the Great Powers announced, the treaty signatories would be limited to newly created states and to states greatly expanded as a result of the war. In other words, no concessions on minority rights would be required from established states, not even from Germany, which, though vanquished, was certainly "established." Clemenceau explained the procedure to Polish Prime Minister Ignacy Jan Paderewski, whose country would be ordered to sign. "It had become a recognized principle of European international custom," Clemenceau wrote, "that in Eastern Europe the establishment of new states . . . required the formal recognition of the Great Powers." And in 1919 the Supreme Council called on that precedent to justify its limited list of signatories. The announcement should have come as no surprise.

At the opening session Clemenceau had declared that the supreme authority for all decision making would rest with the Great Powers, who had sacrificed twelve million men. Wilson continued to assert, "Where the great force lies, there must be the sanction of peace."[18]

Besides, when it came to minority rights, the alternatives were unacceptable. The Great Powers had not assembled in Paris to settle issues they had largely ignored at home, nor would they extend negotiations into imperial domains.[19] As historian H. W. V. Temperley observed, if members of the Supreme Council had put themselves on the same footing with smaller states, it could have been interpreted "in such a way as to bring the Negroes in the Southern States of America under the protection of the League," and "it could have been applied to the Basques of Spain, to the Welsh, and to the Irish."[20] This was no secret in 1919. Queen Marie of Romania, on a visit to Paris, took up the question with Wilson. "He very sanctimoniously preached to me how we should treat our minorities," the queen later wrote, but when she "mildly suggested" that Wilson must be "acquainted with the difficulties [of minority rights] because of the Negro and Japanese questions in the United States," the president responded by baring "his rather long teeth" and declaring "that he was not aware there was a Japanese question in America."[21] The same world leaders who had rejected Japan's request for a "racial equality" provision in the League Covenant were not about to embrace a global definition of "minority rights."

Accusing the Supreme Council of acting like a reconstituted Congress of Vienna, the Romanian and Yugoslav delegates led a short-lived revolt against the treaties. Nikola Pašić, head of the Serb-Croat-Slovene delegation, insisted on the good faith of the "lesser nations" and explained that Yugoslavia, "composed of a single people with three names, three religions, and two alphabets, by its very nature [was] called to practice the broadest tolerance." Pašić also questioned the definition of "new states" and demanded that minority rights clauses be applied, if they must be applied, only to recently acquired lands and not to the historic core of Serbia.[22] Even more violent opposition came from the Romanian Ion I. C. Bratianu, widely acknowledged as the most "ruthless" delegate at the conference (he performed "like a peddler in an oriental bazaar," said one French official). References to Romania's miserable treatment of its Jews caused Bratianu to go red with anger "to the roots of his hair," but another issue rankled most. Demanding to know why the treaties were selectively applied, Bratianu reminded the Great Powers of their pledge that "no nation should seek to extend its policy over any other nation or people" (as Wilson had put it in the midst of the war), and he challenged the American president to deliver on the promise that the "select classes of mankind" would no longer be "the governors of mankind." The more Bratianu protested, however, the more Clemenceau affirmed his belief in the "real differences" between the "characters" of the East European and the West European peoples. "You are here to listen," the French premier shouted at the Romanian, "not to comment!"[23]

Resistance to the minority rights provisions of "the dictated peace" continued through the fall of 1919, but the "lesser nations" had no choice but to sign. Yugoslavia accepted its treaty on 5 December, and four days later, after winning minor concessions on clauses dealing with Jewish rights, the Romanian delegation signed its part of the Treaty of Trianon.[24] Minority clauses, with variations, were also signed by Poland, Czechoslovakia, Greece, Austria, Bulgaria, Hungary, Turkey, and other states. Conceived in the spring of 1919 with the purpose of ending violence in Eastern and Central Europe, the treaties came to official life in an atmosphere of cynicism and hostility. For the populations they were designed to protect, however, they represented the hope that the international community would intervene in the defense of defenseless minorities.

For a short time, the League of Nations attempted to do just that. The Covenant's Article XI established the right of any nation to call the attention of all to "any circumstances anywhere which threaten to disturb international peace or the good understanding between nations." Those circumstances included minority grievances, and any League member could petition the Supreme Council and call for an investigation and remedy on behalf of a minority.[25] Furthermore, in late 1920, the Tittoni report, in a significant revision of the existing system, gave minorities the right to appeal directly to an international body. In Geneva the Minorities Council received hundreds of petitions concerning the treatment of racial, linguistic, and religious minorities. Though some were rejected on technical grounds and many were handled through compromise, still others, such as the grievances of German minorities in Poland, were submitted to the Permanent Court of International Justice, with positive results.[26]

But the minorities system suffered a series of "irreparable" blows that began with the failure of the United States to join the League of Nations. Wilson's political opponents welcomed the ammunition provided by the hyphenated American protesters who came to Capitol Hill. Angered that minority rights had not been extended to the oppressed peoples of the British Empire, Irish-Americans attacked Wilson (their "pathetic" chief executive) and announced, "The world . . . is beginning to realize what Wellington meant when he said after Waterloo, 'There is only one thing worse than defeat—victory.'" Egyptian-Americans, Persian-Americans, and others echoed the protests against imperialism, while the Hungarian-American Press Association, concerned about the treatment of Magyar minorities in Romania, Czechoslovakia, and Yugoslavia, repeated the Hungarian slogan against the Treaty of Trianon: *"nem, nem, soha!"* ("no, no, never!"). Embittered and grandiloquent, Bela Sekely, like so many other testifiers, told the congressional committee that the "League of injustice" was "Lucifer masquerading as the Angel of Paris" and that in its covenant one could discover the "unmistakable signs of satanic majesty."[27]

Four years later, in 1923, the most striking violation of the new principle of international protection for minorities emerged as part of the Balkans peace settlement. Citing the impossibility of protecting besieged minorities in hostile lands, the Lausanne Conference approved a bilateral agreement calling for the compulsory exchange of Greek and Turkish populations. Approximately 1.5 million Greeks and 500,000 Turks were transferred across borders—some willingly, others forcibly, and all as symbols of a minorities rights system that had broken down. In historian Eric Hobsbawm's words, the mass expulsions of the interwar years represented "the murderous *reductio ad absurdum* of nationalism in its territorial version."[28]

But nothing in the 1919 treaties made those actions inevitable. Population transfers and, eventually, genocide emerged as "solutions" to minorities problems not because of inadequate paperwork in Paris but because of the abdication of the political and moral will to confront tyrants and to make the treaties function. The fact that the League system never had an effective mechanism to enforce decisions was the fault (or the calculation) of the political leadership of the interwar years. One spokesman for the Slovenes in Italy summarized the dilemma of the 1930s: "Although the present system of international minorities protection is still valid in a legal sense, politically it is in a state of dissolution and cannot be saved through appeals to the League of Nations."[29]

In 1934, barely one year after Adolf Hitler's seizure of power and at the height of his crusade against the Versailles treaty, the General Assembly of the League of Nations held its last major discussion of minority rights. The minorities treaties, designed at their inception to end violence against East European Jews, were all but dead at the age of fifteen.

Universal Human Rights and Ethnic Tensions

The treaties' official obituary had to await another world war. In December 1947, the UN Human Rights Commission launched a study of the minorities treaties, and three years later the secretariat declared the obvious. Circumstances had "changed to such an extent" that the League system of international protection "should be considered as having ceased to exist."[30] The UN aimed to replace the existing system, which had been designed to protect minorities as groups, with international agreements guaranteeing the rights of all individuals, a process that began with the Universal Declaration of Human Rights (adopted in 1948 as a "common standard of achievement for all peoples and all nations") and that eventually informed the Helsinki Accords. To a great extent, the shift to a "universalist" approach was inspired by the failure of the 1919 treaties, as well as by the experience of the Nuremberg Trials. In 1945–46 individuals were not held responsible under international law, a fact that made the war crimes trials technically "extralegal." That would change. And though the Genocide Convention of 1948 would affirm the most fundamental group right of all—the right of minorities to survive—the trend of the post–World War II era led away from the official recognition of group entities.[31]

Moreover, for clear and tragic reasons, the numbers of national minorities within existing European states had declined dramatically. The deportation of unwanted immigrants, the extermination of peoples by totalitarian regimes, and the movement of populations immediately after World War II (including the expulsion of three million Sudeten Germans from Czechoslovakia) created a Europe in which barely 8 percent of the population were national minorities. After World War I, that number had exceeded 30 percent.[32]

But in the wake of 1991, with the dissolution of another twen-tieth-century empire and a new flood tide of immigration, the numbers changed again. In Central and Eastern Europe, the cold war that had frozen physical boundaries had also frozen the mi-norities question. When the thaw came, nationalist desires born in the nineteenth century and given a short breath of life after 1918 reemerged like a perverse "Sleeping Beauty" (as the presi-dent of Estonia put it), with all "the prewar passions and atti-tudes" of the suppressed countries intact.[33] The Baltic states separated from their former Russian masters; other parts of the Soviet Empire proclaimed forms of autonomy and indepen-dence; and across Europe the question of what to do with the "disturbed spirits" of national minorities returned. In 1993 nearly twenty-five million of those minorities were ethnic Rus-sians, with problems ranging from property rights and second-class political status in the Baltics to murderous ethnic violence in Moldova, Georgia, and Tajikistan. Poor, desperate, and ready to fight for their ethnic neighbors, Russian troops still linger in many regions where five decades of scores remain unsettled. The minorities question continues to be an unresolved item on Boris Yeltsin's crisis-ridden agenda.[34]

The "permanent solution" of Yugoslavia, as one American put it in 1919, has revealed its impermanence, and minority popula-tions in the new Balkan republics require protection. Given the intensity of hatred and the unequal firepower, it is not likely that the sovereign governments will move, without prodding, to-ward a meaningful system of minority rights. "It is tempting to think that [threats to minorities] can be allayed by giving con-stitutional guarantees," one journalist recently observed, "but any government prepared to undertake ethnic cleansing by bazooka is unlikely to be deterred by a few clauses in a consti-tution."[35] In the short term, however, such governments may be deterred by counterforce. Strong action taken by the North At-lantic Treaty Organization (NATO) and the UN early in 1994 saved Sarajevo from annihilation; and by midsummer of the fol-lowing year, approximately twenty-three thousand UN troops were in place in Bosnia and over twelve thousand in Croatia. The region's former UN high commissioner for refugees had warned that "with no one watching," the bloodshed would start anew; but well into 1995, with the world watching, the blood-shed never stopped. UN peacekeepers were taken hostage, and UN-designated "safe areas" fell or were threatened. As Carl

Bildt, the European Union's peace mediator, put it, "these so-called safe areas" were never demilitarized or defended "in the way required by the glorious resolution of the UN Security Council." When Croatia reentered the conflict with a massive push into the Serb-held Krajina region in July 1995, tens of thousands more refugees were set adrift. New initiatives aimed to provide besieged minorities with some sort of "protective envelope"; as 1995 drew to a close, the Dayton peace plan secured that protection for the moment at least. When UN troops gave way to NATO's "implementation force" (Ifor) the estimated number of people displaced since the war began approached four million.[36]

To a certain extent, economic sanctions, though not always effective weapons in the battle for human rights, undermined the alliance of the Serbian president Slobodan Milošević and the Bosnian Serb leader Radovan Karadžić. In 1994, feeling the effects of the international trade embargo, Milošević criticized his comrade for refusing to sign a UN-brokered peace plan that both Croatia and Bosnia had accepted in principle. But while those leaders disagreed over the timing and tactics of war and peace, they also remained, like Bratianu at the Paris Peace Conference, fierce critics of international intervention in the domain of minority rights. A senior U.S. State Department official had territorial nationalists like Milošević and Karadžić in mind when he remarked, with more hope than expectation, "We have to get away from the idea of total respect for sovereignty that was once sacrosanct."[37]

Farther north in Europe, Slovaks have separated from Bohemians and Moravians in a divorce that has been relatively tranquil, though the Sudeten problem continues to trouble the Czech government, and minority grievances remain part of a "fiery controversy" in Slovakia, where many of that country's six hundred thousand ethnic Hungarians fear the consequences of a resurgent Slovak "national consciousness." A recent dam project heightened tensions when it uprooted ethnic Hungarians along a stretch of the Danube River, and in the summer of 1993 Hungarians protested the government order that no language other than Slovak be used in birth registers and on signs of geographic locations. In that case, however, outside pressure resolved the conflict. Young Slovakia's concern for its international reputation, along with its desire to join the Council of Europe (an organization that requires each state to sign the European

Convention of Human Rights), outweighed its interest in linguistic purity. The registers and placards now meet with Hungarian approval. If the example is minor, the lesson is not. When the carrot is sweet enough or the stick big enough, sovereign nations will act, to some degree at least, on minority rights.[38]

U.S. Secretary of State Warren Christopher attempted to stress that point at the World Conference on Human Rights held in Vienna in June 1993. "Those who desecrate . . . fundamental human rights, especially those of minorities," Christopher told the representatives of 155 governments, "must know that they will be ostracized. They will face sanctions. They will be brought before tribunals of international justice. They will not gain access to investment or assistance. And they will not gain acceptance by the community of civilized nations." Earlier Christopher had proposed a new "international tribunal" for aggrieved minorities, a tribunal that would go beyond the Permanent Court, where only claims between states are addressed, and that would (though the secretary never made the connection) resemble the Geneva-based Minorities Council of the post–World War I era. Moreover, in contrast to Wilson in Paris, Christopher in Vienna recognized the perils of special treatment for Great Powers. "No nation can claim perfection" on the question of human rights, Christopher announced, "not the United States nor any other nation." And finally, in the new spirit of "assertive multilateralism," the administration of President Bill Clinton embraced the idea of greater U.S. military involvement in UN peacekeeping. Defense Secretary William Perry toned down his early enthusiasm for a "multinational expeditionary force," but with more than a dozen UN peacekeeping forces currently in place around the globe, it is clear that we are seeing "the haphazard creation of an embryonic international army."[39]

The groundwork for increased protection of minorities has been partially laid, but there remains a lack of agreement on the appropriate mission of the UN. From the outset, UN doctrine, much like that of the League of Nations, defined aggression against any member as aggression against all members, and it called for multinational forces to fight alongside the victim. But that "part of UN doctrine," one observer has written, "never made it to Bosnia." Rather than taking a strong stand in defense of a recognized member state, world leaders, in an attempt to placate all factions, stressed the "impartiality" of international forces at work in the Balkans. This was not the behavior that Wilson, a realist when it came to "great force" and the "sanction of peace," envisioned in his new society of nations; this was not the original idea of "collective security" designed by the UN.[40]

Meanwhile, members of the European Union are sending peacekeepers into global trouble zones but cannot agree on a cohesive, long-term program to protect minorities. "Coherence is the key," insists Carl Bildt. "There are no separate national political moves that are credible." At the same time, yet another "minorities crisis" is intensifying across Europe as immigrant populations multiply and economies stagnate. Between 1980 and 1992, fifteen million immigrants flooded into Western Europe, and they continue to arrive at a rate of more than one million a year. Over the last decade, the number of asylum-seekers has risen tenfold. In 1992 alone, more than 400,000 people sought asylum in Germany, and, in addition, 250,000 refugees arrived as victims of the Bosnian war. The only beneficiaries of that vast human tragedy have been the political parties of the Far Right— the Republican Party in Germany, the National Front in France, the Freedom Party in Austria, the Vlaams Blok in Belgium, and so on down the line of organized xenophobes. In response to the dual pressures of demagoguery and demographics, the governments of Germany and France have tightened immigration laws and conditions for asylum. In 1993 the French interior minister announced a goal of "zero immigration."[41]

Debates over the very definitions of "minority rights" and "human rights" divide the international community. In the universalist spirit of the UN declaration, most observers believe that "rights are best thought of as inherent in each human being, irrespective of what kind of cultural grouping he or she may belong to."[42] But many critics, often from states with deplorable human rights records, equate universalism with an attitude that is ignorant of diverse cultures and often hostile to them. At the Vienna Conference and in UN deliberations, China, Cuba, Pakistan, Iran, Syria, and other nations have asserted that the definition of "human rights" must take into account "national and regional particularities and various historical, cultural, and religious backgrounds."[43] Furthermore, challenging the threat of economic sanctions, they insist that the right to development is inalienable and that aid must not be linked to the question of human rights.

Delegates at Vienna debated these issues and summarized their findings in a "Declaration and Programme of Action." A number of passages addressed the topic of minority rights, including one that resonated with the language of the "model" document of the twentieth century, the 1919 Polish treaty. "Persons belonging to minorities have the right to enjoy their own culture, to profess and practice their own religions, and to use their own language in private and in public, freely and without interference or any form of discrimination."[44] For many national minorities, from Francophones in Canada to Hungarians in the Banat, issues of education and cultural identity are as pressing now as they were in the aftermath of World War I. The Vienna declaration suggests that the Polish treaty is being "dusted off" (in Charles S. Maier's words) as a blueprint for the post–cold war era.[45] The Vienna Conference also called for the channeling of greater resources to the UN Center for Human Rights and reaffirmed the obligation of states to act in accordance with the UN "Declaration on the Rights of Persons Belonging to the National or Ethnic, Religious, and Linguistic Minorities."

Across the decades since 1919, as new groups have entered the political arena, as the definition of "minorities" has expanded, and above all, as the scale of human violence has escalated, the candidates for protection have multiplied. Along with disabled persons, victims of toxic waste dumping, and all individuals whose "dignity" might be endangered by "certain advances in the biomedical and life sciences," the Vienna Conference noted most prominently the worldwide increase in violence against women and girl-children. "The human rights of women and of the girl-child are an inalienable, integral, and indivisible part of universal human rights," the declaration announced. On that topic at least, it went on to challenge the argument of cultural relativists: "Gender-based violence and all forms of sexual harassment and exploitation, including those resulting from cultural prejudice and international trafficking, are incompatible with the dignity and worth of the human person and must be eliminated."[46] But if the words could not be stronger, the provisions for policing—for effectively responding to systematic rape, ritual mutilation, sexual slavery, dowry deaths, and other abuses—could not be weaker. On those issues and others, the Vienna delegates rarely ventured from the abstract to the concrete. Nor did they agree on the creation of a UN High Commissioner for Human Rights. That proposal, associated with the Western powers, was dropped into the chasm of ideological division and was sent back to the UN General Assembly for "consideration."

"More identities asserted," political scientist Michael Walzer tells us, "more rights demanded, more organizations in the field, more people shouting (in new accents). All this points toward a more tumultuous politics."[47] And given the revolutionary development of communications in the decades since 1919, "all this" also points toward the greater flow of information from minorities under siege to international human rights groups and monitoring bodies. As one scholar notes, wireless technologies "eliminate the dependence upon governmentally controlled lines of communication," and they provide, literally and figuratively, one of the most striking contrasts between this century's two "new world orders."[48] The Great Powers in Paris often struggled to gather hard evidence on which to act (or not); they tried to unravel the realities and rumors of minority crises in faraway lands. But the world leaders of the satellite age, immediate witnesses to global atrocities, cannot call on the excuse of ignorance.

The tumult of minority demands, the constant shouting "in new accents," also provokes a reactionary search for stability in an unfragmented world. Neo-Nazis and skinheads across Europe "listen to the speeches of ideologues who hark back to a bygone era when their countries were supposedly homogeneous, comfortable . . . and virtually all white." Jean-Marie Le Pen in France and his counterparts elsewhere in Europe wave the warning flag of "cultural invasion" and job competition and gain the support of fearful populations. From Britain to Russia, a powerful far-right brand of "retrospective mythology" offers the seductive promise of a world without minorities.[49]

Less powerful, because built on the complicated premise of tolerance rather than on the simple foundation of force, is the current cottage industry of nostalgia for the multicultural, multinational Austro-Hungarian Empire. "The break-up of the Habsburg empire," Gellner has noted, "was absolutely catastrophic in its consequences," leading, as it did, to the domination of Central and Eastern Europe, first by Hitler and then by Joseph Stalin.[50] Novels, films, and museum exhibitions—some of them eloquent, many of them frivolous—portray the cosmopolitan atmosphere of Vienna and Budapest on the eve of the Great War. The significance of that nostalgia lies in its attempt to retrieve the memory of a Europe before Sarajevo, Auschwitz, and Sarajevo again. Of course the Habsburg Empire, with its dependent populations and vast inequities, was never a harmonious polity of multiculturalism ("a grand house full of doors and rooms for all sorts of people," in the selective memory of novelist Joseph

Roth);[51] Czechs had it better than Gypsies, Hungarians better than Czechs, and German-speaking Austrians better than them all. Yet nostalgia, like stereotyping, needs a fundamental reality to distort. Europe before World War I, like Yugoslavia before 1991, was a working assembly of diverse peoples who, despite deep prejudices and bitter rivalries, had not yet exercised the option of systematically killing each other on the altar of ethnic nationalism.

The historical record of the Paris Peace Conference and the first new world order of the twentieth century is set. We know the sincerity of some treaty-makers and the cynicism of others; we know the consequences of the bad diplomacy and failure of will. With Europe's newest order still in the making, it remains unclear how the international community will apply the lessons of 1919 and the interwar years—how it will deal with the fragmentation of self-determination, with the enduring demons of nationalism, and with the plight of new minorities. The record since 1991 is encouraging up to a point. In the former Yugoslavia, international intervention has cracked the carapace of national sovereignty and, with a massive arsenal, forced the separation of warring factions. The civilian dimension of the peace plan, however, has yet to address Georges Clemenceau's "complex art" of arranging how minority populations in hostile lands are to secure protection and live in peace.

Notes

[1] Oswald Garrison Villard, *Fighting Years: Memoirs of a Liberal Editor* (New York: Harcourt Brace, 1939), 447; Interview with President Jimmy Carter, *USA Today*, 14 June 1993. See also Arno J. Mayer, *Politics and Diplomacy of Peacemaking: Containment and Counterrevolution at Versailles* (New York: Knopf, 1967), which remains one of the most thorough accounts of the conference in its broad European context.

[2] Daniel Patrick Moynihan, *Pandaemonium: Ethnicity in International Politics* (Oxford: Oxford University Press, 1993), 147 and passim; "States of Mind," *Time*, 1 February 1993, 40. For contemporary assessments, see Amitai Etzioni, "The Evils of Self-Determination," *Foreign Policy* 89 (Winter 1992–93): 35, and Charles Gati, "From Sarajevo to Sarajevo," *Foreign Affairs* 71 (Fall 1992): 64–78.

[3] Ernest Gellner, comments, at international conference "New European Orders: 1919 and 1991," Central European University, Prague, Czech Republic, 17 June 1993.

[4] Woodrow Wilson, quoted in H. W. V. Temperley, ed., *A History of the Peace Conference of Paris*, 6 vols. (London: H. Frowde, Hodder and Stoughton, 1920–24), 4:429. On Robert Lansing's comments, see Moynihan, *Pandaemonium*, 84, and

David Binder and Barbara Crossette, "As Ethnic Wars Multiply, U.S. Strives for a Policy," *New York Times*, 7 February 1993.

[5] Robert W. Seton-Watson, *A History of the Czechs and Slovaks* (Hamden, Conn.: Archon, 1965), 327; Jacob Robinson et al., *Were the Minorities Treaties a Failure?* (New York: Antin, 1943), 35.

[6] Frances Deák, *Hungary at the Paris Peace Conference* (New York: Columbia University Press, 1942), 208; Sherman Spector, *Rumania at the Paris Peace Conference: A Study of the Diplomacy of Ion I. C. Bratianu* (New York: Bookman, 1962), 227; Temperley, *History of the Peace* 5:126–28; Adalbert Toth and Jean Berenger in *Les Conséquences des Traités de Paix de 1919-1920 en Europe Centrale et Sud-Orientale*, ed. Pierre Aycoberry, Jean-Paul Bled, and Istvan Hunyadi (Strasbourg: Universités de Strasbourg, 1987), 156, 161.

[7] Temperley, *History of the Peace* 5:121.

[8] Boutros Boutros-Ghali, "Don't Make the U.N.'s Job Harder," *New York Times*, 20 August 1993.

[9] Michael Walzer, "Between Nation and World," *Economist*, 11–17 September 1993, 49–52.

[10] Georges Clemenceau, *Grandeurs et misères d'une victoire* (Paris: Plon, 1930), 149–50.

[11] Lawrence Gelfand, *The Inquiry: American Preparations for Peace, 1917–1919* (New Haven: Yale University Press, 1963), 16, 158, 216–19, 330.

[12] Voirica Moisuc and Jean Berenger in *Les Conséquences*, 66, 162; Charles Homer Haskins and Robert Howard Lord, *Some Problems of the Peace Conference* (Cambridge, Mass.: Harvard University Press, 1920), 210. See also Paul Birdsall, *Versailles Twenty Years After* (Hamden, Conn.: Archon, 1962), 7–8: "Austria-Hungary had fallen apart before the Peace Conference convened and *de facto* national governments rule the pieces."

[13] *The Papers of Woodrow Wilson*, ed. Arthur S. Link, 69 vols. (Princeton: Princeton University Press, 1966–94), 57:343–45 and 59:198, 419, 445, 514; Janusz Zarnowski in *Les Conséquences*, 196.

[14] Nathan Feinberg, *La Question des minorités à la Conférence de la Paix de 1919-1920 et l'action juive en faveur de la protection internationale des minorités* (Paris: Rousseau, 1929), 19, 32–34, and passim; James Wycliffe Headlam-Morley, *A Memoir of the Paris Peace Conference, 1919* (London: Methuen, 1972), 55–59, 113, and passim; Marc Vichniac, *La Protection des droits des minorités dans les traités internationaux de 1919–1920* (Paris: n.p., 1920), 26–27; Temperley, *History of the Peace* 5:123; Émile Joseph Dillon, *The Inside Story of the Peace Conference* (New York: Harper and Bros., 1920), 12–13; *Comité des délégations juives auprès de la conférence de la paix* (Paris: n.p., 1919–20), 7–9 and passim.

[15] See *The Peace Conference, Paris, 1919: Report of the Delegation of the Jews of the British Empire* (London: n.p., 1920); Feinberg, *Question des minorités*, 71–72; Eugene C. Black, "Squaring the Minorities Triangle" (unpublished paper) 1987.

[16] Robinson, *Were the Minorities*, 35–37, 236–38; Feinberg, *Question des minorités*, 11–12, 130, 141–45.

[17] Temperley, *History of the Peace* 5:113–17; Feinberg, *Question des minorités*, 15–16; Robinson, *Were the Minorities*, 39; József Galántai, *Trianon and the Protec-*

tion of Minorities, trans. Ervin Dunay (Boulder, Colo.: Social Science Monographs, 1992), 33–37.

[18] *Papers of Woodrow Wilson* 59:646; Spector, *Rumania*, 67–114; Robinson, *Were the Minorities*, 162–64; Dillon, *Inside Story*, 475; Feinberg, *Question des minorités*, 11–20, 165; Temperley, *History of the Peace* 5:116.

[19] One high-ranking British diplomat summarized it best: "Would you apply self-determination to India, Egypt, Malta, and Gibraltar?," he asked a subaltern. "If you are *not* prepared to go as far as this, then you have no right to claim that you are logical. If you *are* prepared to go as far as this," the diplomat concluded, "then you had better return at once to London" (Sir Eyre Crowe to Harold Nicolson, quoted in Charles L. Mee, Jr., *The End of Order: Versailles, 1919* [New York: Dutton, 1980], 37).

[20] Temperley, *History of the Peace* 5:142; see also Dillon, *Inside Story*, 503–4.

[21] On the queen's visit, see Spector, *Rumania*, 111–12.

[22] Nikola Pašić, quoted in Galántai, *Trianon*, 74; see also Ivo J. Lederer, *Yugoslavia at the Paris Peace Conference: A Study in Frontiermaking* (New Haven: Yale University Press, 1963), 239, and Robinson, *Were the Minorities*, 154–58.

[23] Spector, *Rumania*, 18, 29, 67, 81–85; Robinson, *Were the Minorities*, 5, 161; Hamilton Foley, *Woodrow Wilson's Case for the League of Nations* (New York: Kraus Reprints, 1969), 212–16; *Papers of Woodrow Wilson* 59:646.

[24] Vichniac, *La Protection*, 30–31; Temperley, *History of the Peace* 5:149.

[25] Charles S. Maier, "Unsafe Haven," *New Republic*, 12 October 1992, 21.

[26] Robinson, *Were the Minorities*, 57, 85–87, 261; Galántai, *Trianon*, x, 117–18; Robert Gascoyne-Cecil, *A Great Experiment* (London: J. Cape, 1941), 118–20.

[27] *Treaty of the Peace with Germany*, 66th Cong., 1st sess., 1919, S. Doc. 76, serial 7608, 754, 873, 889, 928; Robinson, *Were the Minorities*, 58; Berenger in *Les Conséquences*, 159. Joining those critics were former supporters of Woodrow Wilson on the Left—internationalists, pacifists, socialists, and progressive liberals—who, by the summer of 1919, were condemning the peace process as a breach of faith. Forgotten was the fact that Wilson had been the standard-bearer in Paris for minority rights; remembered was the unfulfilled promise of a "new departure" from old diplomacy (see Thomas J. Knock, *To End All Wars: Woodrow Wilson and the Quest for a New World Order* [New York: Oxford University Press, 1992]).

[28] Eric Hobsbawm, *Nations and Nationalism since 1780: Programme, Myth, Reality* (Cambridge: Cambridge University Press, 1990), 132–34; Robinson, *Were the Minorities*, 57; Galántai, *Trianon*, 89.

[29] Vichniac, *La Protection*, 64; Robinson, *Were the Minorities*, 253, 263.

[30] Quoted in Galántai, *Trianon*, 140.

[31] Philip Alston, "The United Nation's Human Rights Record: From San Francisco to Vienna and Beyond," *Human Rights Quarterly* 16 (1994): 375–90. The Helsinki Final Act of 1977 confirmed the right to "self-determination," and the Copenhagen Agreements of 1990, in landmark language, explicitly called for the protection of national minorities (Professor Herman Schwartz, comments, Woodrow Wilson International Center for Scholars, Washington, D.C., March 1993). But the universalist approach dominated the post-1945 era.

[32] Michael R. Marrus, *The Unwanted: European Refugees in the Twentieth Century* (New York: Oxford University Press, 1986).

[33] Steven Erlanger, "Baltic Identity: Russians Wonder If They Belong," *New York Times*, 22 November 1992.

[34] Ibid.; see also Francis Fukuyama, "Trapped in the Baltics," *New York Times*, 19 December 1992, and Editorial, *New York Times*, 1 August 1993. George Soros discusses the violence in the former Soviet Union and elsewhere in "Bosnia and Beyond," *New York Review of Books*, 7 October 1993, 15–16.

[35] "When Countries Splinter," *Economist*, 12 June 1992, 11; see also "The Serbs' Next Target?," *Economist*, 29 May 1993, 54, on the crisis of ethnic Albanians in the Kosovo province of southern Serbia.

[36] Carl Bildt, "We Cannot Walk Away," *Financial Times*, 21 July 1995; "Tide of Refugees Turns into Flood," *Financial Times*, 9 August 1995; and "Victims of Bosnian Realpolitik," *Economist*, 22 July 1995, 47–48. The former UN official is quoted in Chuck Sudetic, "In Bosnia Again, a Grim 'Ethnic Cleansing,'" *New York Times*, 17 February 1994.

[37] Binder and Crossette, "As Ethnic Wars Multiply"; see also Soros, "Bosnia and Beyond."

[38] Amy Auster, "Slovakia Caves In on Hungarian," *Prague Post*, 16–22 June 1993.

[39] "Democracy and Human Rights: Where America Stands," remarks delivered by U.S. Secretary of State Warren Christopher, Vienna, Austria, World Conference on Human Rights, 14 June 1993. On "assertive multilateralism," see R. Jeffrey Smith and Julia Preston, "U.S. to Widen UN Peace Role," *International Herald Tribune*, 19–20 June 1993, and former National Security Adviser Brent Scowcroft's comments in "Who Can Harness History?: Only the U.S.," *New York Times*, 2 July 1993. And on a standing UN army, see Kai Bird, "Humanitarian Intervention: The Case of a U.N. Army," *Nation*, 8–15 August 1994.

[40] On this question, see Robert Wright, "Good Ghali," *New Republic*, 15 August 1994, 6.

[41] Bildt, "We Cannot Walk Away." For recent statistics on immigrants and asylum-seekers in Europe, see Craig R. Whitney, "Western Europe's Dreams Turning to Nightmares," *New York Times*, 8 August 1993; see also John Darnton, "Western Europe Is Ending Its Welcome to Immigrants," *New York Times*, 10 August 1993.

[42] Conor Cruise O'Brien, "What Rights Should Minorities Have?," in Ben Whitaker, ed., *Minorities: A Question of Human Rights?* (New York: Pergamon, 1984), 18.

[43] Paul Lewis, "Splits May Dampen Rights Conference," *New York Times*, 6 June 1993.

[44] U.S. Department of State, Bureau of Human Rights and Humanitarian Affairs, *Vienna Declaration and Programme of Action*, 25 June 1993, 9.

[45] Maier, "Unsafe Haven," 20.

[46] U.S. Department of State, *Vienna Declaration*. In 1994, for the first time in its annual human rights report, the U.S. State Department presented data compiled from 193 countries on the "day-to-day discrimination and abuse" of women (see Steven Greenhouse, "U.S. State Department Finds Widespread Abuse of World's Women," *New York Times*, 3 February 1994). On the expanding list of victims of human rights abuses, see Alston's discussion of the six "core"

treaties to which many states now adhere ("The United Nation's Human Rights Record," 376).

[47] Walzer, "Between Nation and World," 51.

[48] Alston, "The United Nation's Human Rights Record," 379.

[49] Darnton, "Western Europe." On nationalism and "retrospective mythology," see Eric Hobsbawm, "Whose Fault-Line Is It Anyway?," *New Statesman and Society*, 24 April 1992, 23–26.

[50] Gellner, comments, "New European Orders."

[51] The quotation is from Joseph Roth's novel *Die Büste des Kaisers* (see the comment by Jean-Paul Bled in *Les Conséquences*, 48–53); for a recent historical analysis, see Alan Sked, *The Decline and Fall of the Hapsburg Empire* (London: Longman, 1989).

Chapter 4

Two Difficult Transitions: Economic Vulnerability after the First World War and after Communism

Charles S. Maier

Statesmen and observers alike turn to historic parallels, no matter how imperfect, for policy guidance. Game-theoretic calculations, for all their amusement value, cannot safely predict likely outcomes because weighting the coefficients that stipulate payoffs and probabilities must remain arbitrary. Knowledge of comparable situations at least seems to add wisdom to guesswork. And only history provides the material for comparison. Whoever ponders policy must turn to historical analogy.

The process of testing the scope of historical analogy (Does it offer one salient parallel or many? Does it also have disabling distinctions? Can the historian weigh the importance of parallels versus differences?) is precisely what gives comparative history its heuristic value. But which analogies should be studied? Most economic analysts focusing on the problems of contemporary Eastern Europe have generally seized on one particular and partial analogy—the period of the Marshall Plan.[1] The fascination is obvious. Policymakers and scholars alike want to decide whether a new Marshall Plan for Eastern Europe could repeat the success of that four-year program in Western Europe after World War II. But the economic situation after World War I is just as instructive and just as close a fit to the contemporary situation.

The 1919 parallel after all involves the same economic region—

Eastern Europe. It features a Russia whose internal economic turmoil precluded any significant regional role and a Germany that was beginning to reassert its industrial and financial power in the region. Now, as in 1919, small states are handicapped by severe economic difficulties, political inexperience, and ethnic conflicts. Finally, the 1919 analogy contains a United States hesitant to exert its own economic power, a situation also akin to the 1990s, although the current American reticence may disappear.

These are powerful and potentially instructive parallels. Any effort to evaluate and draw lessons from the possible analogues must focus on four different dimensions of comparison: first, the persisting difference in development between West and East, a difference that has existed far longer than Communist control; second, the nature of international trade on the eve of the two eras and the nature of the rupture that occurred, first after 1914 and then after 1989—that is, before World War I and before the collapse of the centrally planned economies; third, the patterns of international trade and debt in the two eras; and fourth, the role of labor and migration. Any comparison of the two economic situations must touch on these aspects, no matter how briefly. Moreover, in thinking about the economic situation of 1919 and that of 1989, the historian must consider two overlapping arenas. The first is regional and concerns the economic difficulties that afflicted Eastern or East-Central Europe after Versailles and again after the collapse of communism. The second is broader and concerns the world economy, or certainly that of the advanced industrial societies. To what extent did World War I contribute to the overall lackluster economic performance before and during the Great Depression? Does the world economy confront similar problems, and if so, why? Clearly, one major difference between the two eras is that the post-Communist era has not come as the aftermath of a great and devastating war. For that reason alone, there may be more robustness and less vulnerability today. On the other hand, there may be other sources of fragility. Ultimately this comparison should reveal where they may lie.

Too Much, Too Late: Legacies of Backwardness

There is a similarity between the situations of East-Central Europe and Russia: a backwardness relative to the countries of the

TABLE 1

PERCENTAGE OF LABOR FORCE IN AGRICULTURE

Country	1930–34	1950	1970	1979
Czechoslovakia	28	17	—	—
Poland	65	56	—	23
Bulgaria	80	70	70–74	24
Yugoslavia	79	68	47	—
Romania	78	74	49	31

Source: Nina Watt, "Eastern and Western Europe," in Andrea Boltho, ed., *The European Economy: Growth and Crisis* (New York: Oxford University Press, 1982), 261 (table 9.2); Alice Teichova, "East-Central and South-East Europe, 1919–39," in Peter Mathias and Sidney Pollard, eds., *Cambridge Economic History of Europe*, 2d ed., vol. 8 (Cambridge: Cambridge University Press, 1966–89), 891 (table 121); John R. Lampe and Marvin R. Jackson, *Balkan Economic History, 1550–1950* (Bloomington: Indiana University Press, 1982), 597 (table 14.2).

West. Until the mid-twentieth century, the lands of Eastern Europe had far larger agricultural sectors with lower productivity. At the outbreak of World War I, industrial development was advanced in Bohemia and was increasing rapidly in Russia, but it still lagged behind that of the West. As the percentage of the population employed in agriculture and fishing reveals, this situation did not change until after 1950 (see table 1). In 1930 only Czechoslovakia had an occupational profile comparable to that of West European societies.

Moreover, the East European agricultural sector was unmechanized and poor. Its productivity was low because most peasant farms were too small for effective exploitation. The land reforms carried out in Eastern Europe during the 1920s could not address the problems of dwarf holdings; indeed, the reforms tended to aggravate them.[2] Poor peasants could not provide a robust market for industrial products, and an underdeveloped industry could not absorb excess labor from the countryside. Agricultural prices fell (except in the late 1920s), and Eastern Europe, together with parts of the American South and Latin America, remained a stagnant backwater of misery. This failure to prosper was reflected in that revealing index of social well-being, the infant mortality rate (see table 2).

Russian and East European backwardness persisted until well after World War II. In Western Europe, by contrast, the modernization of the countryside was already well under way at the end of World War II and was essentially completed in France, Germany, and the Netherlands by the early 1960s. French wheat pro-

TABLE 2

DEATHS OF INFANTS UNDER ONE YEAR OF AGE (LIVE BIRTHS PER THOUSAND)

Country	1913	1929	1960
Sweden	71	59	17
United Kingdom	108	74	22
Germany[a]	151	100	34
Italy	138	125	44
Austria	190	113	38
Hungary	201	179	36
Czechoslovakia	—	142	22
Russia[b]	237	155	35
Bulgaria	133	156	45
Romania	233	197	75
Yugoslavia[c]	139	147	88

Source: B. R. Mitchell, *European Historical Statistics* (London: Macmillan, 1978), A4, 43.

[a]Germany 1960=Federal Republic of Germany.

[b]Russian dates=1911, 1928, 1960.

[c]Yugoslavia 1913=Serbia 1910.

duction doubled between 1946 and the early 1960s; other Western countries made smaller but still significant gains. As agricultural productivity rose, labor migrated from southern Italy and rural France and Holland to urban industries.

The process of agricultural modernization and rural-to-urban migration was more dramatic in Eastern Europe. Postwar Communist rule produced rapid industrialization and economic growth. Under the Stalinist model of central planning—the paradigm of the five-year plan—each of the countries vastly expanded its industrial sector. Even though the investment objectives were increasingly inappropriate, productivity and growth increased until the 1970s and 1980s (see tables 3A and 3B), when they began to fall seriously behind.

Did socialism help Eastern Europe overcome the legacy of backwardness that had been so marked throughout the nineteenth century? In one respect, the answer is "yes." Communist rulers insisted on forcing the industrialization that Western countries had undergone for over a far longer period in the nineteenth century. The Soviet five-year plan—centralized, brutal, often wasteful—became the paradigm for Stalin's epigones in Eastern Europe. The difficulty was that this hectic industrial development in the first two postwar decades did not lead to successive waves of transformation. In terms of services and

TABLE 3A

AVERAGE WEST EUROPEAN GROWTH RATES AFTER WORLD WAR II
(IN TERMS OF GROSS DOMESTIC PRODUCT)

Country	1950–69	1969–79
Federal Republic of Germany	6.2%	3.6%
France	4.9	4.0
Austria	5.0	4.4
Italy	5.4	3.5
Spain	6.1	4.5

TABLE 3B

AVERAGE EAST EUROPEAN GROWTH RATES AFTER WORLD WAR II
(IN TERMS OF GROSS DOMESTIC PRODUCT (GDP)
AND NET MATERIAL PRODUCT (NMP))

Country	1950–69	1969–79
German Democratic Republic	5.7%	4.9%
Hungary	4.8	5.4
Czechoslovakia	5.2	5.1
Poland	6.1	6.3
Bulgaria	6.9	7.3

Note: Figures for 1950–69 reflect changes in GDP; figures for 1969–79 reflect changes in NMP. Countries listed in an order reflecting their approximate individual development.

Source: (for both tables) Compiled from United Nations Economic Commission for Europe (UNECE) and Organization for Economic Cooperation and Development (OECD) statistics by Nina Watt, "Eastern and Western Europe," and data for France derived from Christian Sautter, "France," in Andrea Boltho, ed., *The European Economy: Growth and Crisis* (New York: Oxford University Press, 1982), 262 (table 9.3) and 449 (table 15.1). Comparisons are difficult to make, but the UN statistics are adjusted to include services in the East European economic accounts.

consumer goods, the countries of East-Central Europe remained behind. The Stalinist model, replicated in each communized country, bequeathed a set of investment objectives that might best be described as industrially archaic. Communist planners clung to a "macho" pattern of heavy metal production long after world market conditions and the appearance of new technological opportunities and requirements ceased to indicate that this was a rational allocation of resources. The Asians could make steel cheaply, and the West was shutting down its furnaces, but Eastern Europe paid no heed (see table 4).

The irony was that even as Communist Eastern Europe sought to catch up with the industrial West, the advanced capitalist countries moved on to a different stage of development

TABLE 4

CRUDE STEEL PRODUCTION (IN THOUSANDS OF TONS)

Country	1950	1971	1980	1988
United States	87,848	109,055	101,698	90,012
France	8,652	22,859	23,176	18,598
Federal Republic of Germany	14,019	40,313	43,838	41,023
Japan	4,839	88,557	111,395	105,681
Soviet Union	27,329	120,637	147,931	163,037
Poland	2,515	12,688	19,485	16,872

Source: UNECE, *Quarterly Bulletin of Steel Statistics for Europe* 6, no.1 (Geneva, 1955): 2–13; UNECE, *Annual Bulletin of Steel Statistics for Europe* 8 (1980): 10–11; *Annual Bulletin of Steel Statistics for Europe* 16 (1988): 8–9.

marked by the growth of service industries, information technology, and differentiated consumer goods. In 1914 the countries of Eastern Europe lagged behind the West in terms of industrialization, and their agricultural sectors were far less productive. They never really brought their large agrarian sectors up to Western productivity standards. After World War II, they achieved basic industrialization, only to find that the cutting edge of technological modernization had moved on. Neo-Stalinism was not very good at hitting moving targets.

Communism set out to modernize economies but ultimately reproduced relative backwardness. The error of central planning was that it offered too much too late. Perhaps it might best be regarded as one of a continuing series of state interventions, such as the Petrine or cameralist modernization by "project," that could not overcome the long-term gradient of underdevelopment running from northwest to southeast. This is not to suggest that state interventions were responsible for the persisting backwardness. State interventions were important for infrastructural development, including literacy and education. But they were never able to overcome the four-century burden of bureaucratic empires and "second serfdom."[3]

Disinvestment and Disruptions in the Interwar Decades

The dilemmas currently under discussion among policymakers, however, are not really the persisting deficits of modernization. No one should have expected the Balkans or Eastern Europe suddenly to draw abreast of the West. At issue today, as in 1919, are the acute problems that arise from rapid institutional change. The economies of the new states of 1919 were particularly fragile, as are the economies of the post-Communist states. That "conjunctural" vulnerability is what claims our attention, and the reason for it is not just the accumulated legacy of structural underdevelopment. We must turn from long-term liabilities to crises of the respective decades. Of course, the distinction is not absolute. Ultimately, short-term setbacks or advances determine long-term "structural" trends. The difference between episodes and trends often hinges on the perspective that is chosen.

Both the Eastern Europe of 1919 and that of 1989 experienced a sudden rupture of trade and commercial connections. The regional specialization characteristic of the area has drawbacks as well as virtues. It may facilitate the classical mechanism of comparative advantage, but it also tends to perpetuate the international division of labor. Most societies, unless they control a commodity that commands monopoly prices, such as the Organization of Petroleum Exporting Countries (OPEC) in the 1970s, aspire to develop high value-added activities. Eastern Europe, however, has been repeatedly locked into the disadvantageous situation of supplying primary products or low-technology manufactures. Nevertheless, selling low-tech output is far better than not selling at all.

Before 1914 Germany bought raw materials from Russia and Eastern Europe and sold industrial products and services. So did Britain and France and, to a lesser degree, Italy, which developed markets in the Balkans. Within the Habsburg domains, the Bohemian and Austrian regions exported industrial products, above all textiles and fibers, to the Hungarian realm, which sent its grain to Cisleithania. Even as they bought primary products, the Western powers also provided capital for the development of infrastructure in Eastern Europe—railroads, trams, factories, and banks. Viennese banks dominated both halves of the Dual Monarchy.

This interchange was destroyed by World War I. "Altogether," wrote David Mitrany, "it would be difficult to underestimate the great injury caused to the nonmaterial or potential wealth represented by the delicate organization of trade, and especially for international trade."[4] Russia was removed from international economic exchange by its revolution and civil war. The Habs-

burg domains were fractured, and the previously subject nationalities were suspicious of their former masters. The successor states sought to acquire the direct investments and firms left
by the defeated Central Powers—a policy called nostrification.

It was difficult for the East Europeans to reconstitute their
agricultural markets. The Western Allies were cut off from the
region during the war and turned to Argentine, Canadian, and
American sources of supply. Each country carried out a land reform that often left inefficient and splintered holdings in the
hands of a poor peasantry ripe for political radicalization. Agricultural and commodity prices fell relative to those of industrial
goods until 1924 and again after 1929. Eastern Europe was not
the only region to suffer; so did the American South and the
Japanese countryside. But the stagnation of the East European
countryside and the slow recovery of investment constituted a
major drain on the newly independent countries. Although the
countries of Eastern and Southeastern Europe, including Poland,
maintained their export earnings in the depression, they did so
by tripling the volume of agricultural exports, even as prices fell
by 75 percent.

Ultimately, only Germany was prepared to absorb these exports and then only through bilateral deals that effectively
locked the East European nations into purchases of German armaments and industrial goods. Intra-area trade among the seven
successor states, including Austria, declined from about half the
total trade of these states in the early 1920s to about 36 percent
in 1929 and 23 percent by 1937. Intra-area trade would have been
a healthier alternative than reliance on German bilateral con-
tracts. The latter were part of a larger political goal of hegemonic
penetration, and even if judged purely as economic arrangements, they retarded industrial development in the Danubian region. The exporters of Southeastern Europe had to either provide
credits to Berlin for their exports or pile up reichsmarks in closed
accounts. They also had to absorb German manufactures, which
retarded their industrial development. The French and the
British had a common interest in reducing this reliance on Germany, but the British—equally concerned about the possibility
of French domination of the region through the Little Entente—
were relatively uncooperative in fostering regional trade
schemes.[5]

If commerce stagnated, so did investment. The war destroyed
capital, perhaps half the capital of Europe if we measure by in-

heritances or asset values in real terms. The pervasive postwar inflations were the ill-understood mechanism by which this destruction of capital was apportioned among sectors of the population. For five years after the war, economies did little more than reconstitute some of their losses. The Germans used inflation to recapitalize much of their domestic industry and to try to hold properties in Silesia. The French devoted themselves to rebuilding the northeastern section of their country. By mid-decade these countries were ready to compete in Eastern Europe, and American investors also became active participants. From 1924 to 1929 investment proceeded again, only to dry up in the Great Depression. The depression was just as destructive as the early postwar period and probably should be seen as the delayed aftereffect of war.[6] The war, after all, did lie at the root of more proximate causes such as the continuing weakness of the East European agricultural sector, the failure to develop robust domestic or export markets, and the limits on industrial investment imposed by the gold-exchange standard.[7] The restoration of even a modified gold standard entailed an agreement to repay asset holders (outside the countries where hyperinflation had raged), even at the cost of current production and new net capital formation. As many writers have argued, the gold standard held national policies hostage to high interest rates and deflationary inhibitions.

Moreover, once the depression settled in, it was easier for the Germans to reconstitute economic dominance of the area than it was for the Western powers to do so. Only the Germans were in a position to offer a market for the primary products of Eastern Europe, at the price of locking the countries in as consumers of German industrial goods. Still, French and British interests endeavored to maintain a presence. They effectively took control of important Viennese banks, which became conduits for investment in Eastern Europe. Not all of this foreign investment could go to productive purposes; it also serviced prewar debt, assigned reparations, and military expenditures. Interest rates on foreign loans were about double prewar rates, and domestic industries often had to pay twice again the foreign-loan rate. In 1931 debt service totaled 22 percent of export earnings in Austria, a bit under 30 percent in Romania and Yugoslavia, and 48 percent in Hungary. Only Czechoslovakia's 5 percent was a light burden.[8]

Reviewing the sad record, the historian may be tempted to

ask: were not the handicaps of the interwar East European economy unique in their magnitude? East European societies were still backward and underdeveloped, and their countryside was poor and overcrowded. Abandoned by the West and its wealth, the region had to make its poverty-stricken way in a wider world of depression. Lying between a ravaged Communist economy to the east and a rapacious industrial power to the west, the newly independent states, mutually as jealous as they were needy, were attempting to launch independent national economies in the aftermath of a war that had destroyed whatever capital might have been slowly accumulating. World War I, after all, was a European orgy of disinvestment and squandering. Vigorous investment from 1924 to 1929 began, but only began, to make up for the decade of destruction.

Compared with these burdens, the starting point for the post-Communist economies of 1989 should have been much healthier. Certainly, the apparent record of prior investment and accumulation was more robust. And yet there is a parallel with the situation following World War I. Despite the demands that socialist investment made on current consumption, it was often so divorced from criteria of market efficiency that when the East European economies were exposed to world competition, much of their capital stock was declared worthless. Opening to the West was necessary for the modernization of the socialist economies. But opening to the West also destroyed the value of socialist investment. If ecological devastation is included in this calculation, the situation of 1991 may involve as much disinvestment as that of 1919. The waste of labor resources may be of an equal order of magnitude. Certainly, a large number of workers in socialist factories were as economically unproductive as were soldiers in barracks or on the battlefield. Only uniforms separate conscripts from state-subsidized Kurzarbeiter.

Debits and Credits: The CMEA and the Uses of Suboptimality

Before 1989 the East European economies interacted in a framework of exchange relationships that has since been ruptured. In many ways, the rupture has produced dislocations similar to the breakup of 1919. About 64 percent of Council for Mutual Economic Assistance (CMEA) exports went to other CMEA coun-

TABLE 5

SOVIET OIL PRICES OUTSIDE AND INSIDE THE CMEA

Year	World Mkt. $/ton	Exchange $/ruble	World Mkt. rubles/ton	CMEA rubles/ton
1972	21.4	1.206	17.7	15.7
1974	80.2	1.321	60.9	18.1
1979	142.6	1.526	93.1	63.6
1981	266.7	1.385	192.4	95.0
1983	215.3	1.378	156.3	138.8
1984	215.3	1.378	156.3	156.6*

Source: A. M. Burghardt and C. A. Kortvelyessy, COMECON: Economies, Debt, and Prospects (London: Euromoney Publications, 1984), 31.

*Estimate.

tries in 1970, and that figure was still about 56 percent in 1982.[9] The CMEA, however, was not a trade network that operated on the basis of pure economic rationality, and the reasons for this extend beyond the fact that socialism was less efficient than market capitalism. The CMEA was created to serve Soviet political interests. In return the Soviet Union subsidized CMEA countries by pricing its oil exports on the basis of a five-year moving average of world-market prices. Soviet oil was thus less expensive immediately after the OPEC price increases of 1974 and 1979. By the mid-1980s, however, the five-year moving average pushed Soviet prices to CMEA countries somewhat higher than the by-then declining world-market price, and the countries felt the pinch (see table 5).[10]

Although they grew restive after the mid-1980s as the energy subsidy fell, the CMEA countries still enjoyed access to other inexpensive raw materials, especially iron ore. Most important, they continued to benefit from the arrangement because Moscow paid relatively high prices for manufactured goods. While the Soviets provided cheap oil, they bought Czech, Hungarian, and East German industrial goods that judging from the post-1989 collapse of demand, were probably not tradable in Western markets, certainly not at CMEA prices. Soviet experts themselves understood that they were paying more than necessary and were inhibiting their own investment in manufactures.[11] The result was a subsidized market for manufactures of suboptimal quality, whether these were East German numerically controlled machine tools or Hungarian buses or Polish men's suits. The countries of the Eastern Bloc turned out goods that were not competitive with Western equivalents; the Soviet Union accepted them at inflated prices, then augmented its contribution by providing oil and raw materials at prices below those of the world market.[12]

Why could the CMEA not have continued as a protected enclave of suboptimal make-work production? This is a crucial question for the historian, and I cannot provide a definitive answer. CMEA trade seemed more and more irksome to both sides as Western technology and consumer goods beckoned. The Soviets realized that despite their oil resources, in many cases they were buying second-rate manufactures. The limits of socialist production were increasingly visible. Communist economic performance and capacity for innovation were evidently not only not catching up with the West but actually falling further behind. By the early 1980s, this decline was manifest in areas ranging from competition in computerized weapons to deteriorating public health standards and increasing ecological devastation.

The East Europeans also became disenchanted with CMEA trade, even though they drew significant subsidies from the system. The East German Plan-Kommission archives and the disclosures provided to the final meetings of the central committee in late 1989 reveal the political impact of the massively growing indebtedness to the West. [13] Each CMEA member wanted to buy Western goods. To do so, the member needed to extract convertible currencies from its Eastern Bloc customers. Indeed, Hungary and the Soviet Union reached the first agreement for convertible-currency payments in early 1991, shortly before the whole structure collapsed. But intra-CMEA sales could not generate a net surplus of Western currencies. The CMEA was degenerating into a zero-sum game for shifting the East's overall debt burden to the West. The demand for Western goods far outpaced Communist exports and could be assuaged only by Western credits. While CMEA exports to members of the Organization for Economic Cooperation and Development (OECD) increased only slowly and actually declined as a share of total Western trade, the need to service the massive debts incurred in the 1970s and 1980s was a constant and in some cases increasing pressure. [14]

Industrial Speenhamland though it was, the CMEA at least provided an ongoing system of subsidized employment and access to raw and finished materials. The Trabi and Tatra were not the Volkswagen and Mercedes; the Bulgarian Riviera was not

Cap d'Antibes; a Robitron was not a Compaq; GUM was hardly Bloomingdale's. Still, except for such crises as the Soviet difficulties of 1980–82, and forgetting the ecological time bomb that socialist production had triggered, the CMEA provided a tolerable standard of living. In effect, it functioned like a poor but still viable neighborhood in a large Western city; it had stores with second-rate goods, expensive money lenders, sweatshops, and low-skill labor, but it was better than the alternative of crime, mendicancy, and public assistance.

In fact, the collapse of this admittedly second-rate network of production and exchange has been one of the most distressing aspects of post-1989 conditions in Eastern Europe. This is most dramatically revealed by the plight of East Germany, which, unbelievable as it now seems, once ranked as the world's eleventh major industrial producer. But throughout the region, industrial production has suffered a collapse for which the Great Depression of the early 1930s offers the only peacetime parallel. According to the *Economist*, in the three years from 1990 through 1992, there was a 54-percent decline in industrial production in Bulgaria and Romania, a 40-percent decline in Czechoslovakia, and a 32-percent decline in Hungary and Poland. [15] The United Nations Economic Commission for Europe has recently offered even more sobering statistics: in most of the East European nations, industrial production has fallen to 1975 levels. [16]

Thus, relative economic weakness has been an abiding characteristic of East-Central Europe throughout this century. Economically as well as politically, the countries "in between" have usually become dependent on one of their larger neighbors to construct a framework for regional exchange and development. The rupture of intra-area trade, especially the exchanges within the vanished Dual Monarchy, weakened the small economies after 1918. Further undermined by the subsequent depression and the attrition of the West European economic presence, they had few alternatives to the economic straitjacket offered by National Socialist Germany. Political domination followed economic distress. After World War II, causation ran the other way. Soviet political domination determined the structure of trade and development. The collapse of the CMEA has plunged the area back into the uncoordinated difficulties of 1919. The region has little inherent vibrancy, and its hegemonic neighbors have had little concern for its autonomous development.

The interwar precedent might, therefore, suggest a discouraging prognosis. The interwar economies stagnated and ultimately performed badly enough to undermine the democratic initiatives of 1919. There are significant differences in the two situations, however. Certain lessons have been learned. So far, the former Communist countries, even Russia, have avoided the hyperinflations that destroyed the ruble, the mark, and the Austrian crown and its successors after World War I. Furthermore, in the interwar period, the small countries of Eastern Europe were the object of fierce Great Power rivalry. Even before Adolf Hitler came to power, German political and economic elites used economic power to pursue political hegemony. By contrast, it is encouraging that for now at least, the economies of Eastern Europe are no longer a surrogate battlefield. On the other hand, the disorganization of economic life in Ukraine, Belarus, and Russia does not enhance opportunities for the smaller countries to the west. The prosperity of East-Central Europe requires a larger framework for trade and investment than its own national markets can provide. Mitteleuropa and the CMEA were exploitative in their turn, but they did provide expanded horizons. The hoped-for successor, of course, is the European Union (EU). To a degree, the economic policies of all of the East European states might be described as waiting on Brussels, but Brussels may make them wait a long time.

Both the interwar experience and developments since 1989 suggest that the prosperity of the region as a whole, as well as that of its individual economies, must be targeted. The Czech Republic and Slovenia may fare tolerably well on their own because they have quickly forged links with the West. But capitalism in one country is increasingly difficult. How is the economic future of Eastern Europe as a whole to be best advanced? The advocates of rapid market reforms and privatization—"shock treatment"—have geared their remedies to individual economies, not to the entire region. High unemployment is an immediate consequence of this approach. The great question is: where will the unemployed end up—assembling computers in Krakow, giving permanents in St. Petersburg, or picking pockets in Prague? Emigration has been a traditional answer. One reason for the distress of the interwar period was that the major outlet for surplus labor—the American Midwest—no longer absorbed East European and Russian emigrants because it was closed off for political reasons in 1924. Now too, only German-German migration continues unabated.

Advocates of "shock treatment" tend to assume that the reconstruction of international exchange will follow harmoniously. But more attention may have to be paid to the regional framework in its own right. One alternative would be a more gradual accommodation to Western prices and the interim preservation of a CMEA-like zone, even at the cost of perpetuating second-rate production. The Dienstbier Plan of 1989–90, which called for U.S. funding of Soviet purchases of East European goods, was one variant. Could such a sheltered market of initially second-rate production attract Western investment? How would its factories be weaned from the subsidies? How would they transform themselves into lean and mean state-of-the-art producers concerned with profits rather than jobs?

Extending the concept of the early Dienstbier proposals, another strategy might involve allocating assistance from the United States and the EU to regional projects and to the financing of intraregional trade. From its second year onward, the Marshall Plan provided American dollars to fund European payments agreements and eventually the European Payments Union of 1950. This subsidy encouraged trade among the Europeans, thereby pushing them beyond bilateral exchange. Washington's funds supported not merely European purchases of American commodities but also Italian imports from Britain or French imports from the Netherlands. American aid persuaded the key players who felt they might lose the most from a payments union—Belgium as a strong currency country, Britain as a vulnerable one—to cooperate. A similarly conceived "wasting fund" might provide a temporary inducement to revive intraregional trade, even as the provision for phasing it out over several years could prod modernization.

There is also the question of boundaries. What region will or can be economically redeemed? As in the 1920s, the Czech economy is a vigorous one, oriented toward the West, resistant to inflationary pressures, and developed. Hungary and Poland seem to be coping with the difficulties of transition. But the Balkans, Romania, Ukraine, and Russia face problems of a different magnitude. In contrast to the interwar situation, there is now a West European economic structure that could serve as a plausible framework for internationalizing market solutions. But if it is to have an impact in the East, it must act as a market for the semi-competitive goods of the East. Since the EU is committed to the free movement of capital and labor within its borders, extending trade access alone seems difficult. How much should the EU "broaden" itself? I would argue: more than it has to date. An impoverished Eastern Europe may affect Western economic performance. At the least, continuing poverty in Eastern Europe will increase the appeal of populist xenophobic movements, thereby increasing the number of people seeking to emigrate to the West.

Finally, it is important to recall that twentieth-century economic problems, whether after 1919 or after 1989, involve issues of labor and capital. Labor was radicalized by World War I but was simultaneously coopted into state and managerial hierarchies. Adherents of the new Third International forswore cooperation with liberal capitalist states. The political effects were difficult to manage and had fateful consequences when, at the end of the 1920s, a radicalized farm population made Nazis and Fascists a serious threat. In this respect, outside the Soviet Union at least, there has been a broader ideological consensus in post-1989 politics. If continuing ethnic conflict produces a radical Right, however, more unfortunate parallels with the earlier era may arise. History may not repeat itself, but it does offer a repertory of echoes. And we do hear unsettling echoes of the political appeals that proved so destructive between the wars. By 1930, alas, the evolution of European politics and economics had dashed the hopes of 1919. By the mid-1990s, we have likewise left behind many of the fresh hopes of 1989.

Just a "Transition"?
The Vulnerability of the World Economy

Contemplating Eastern Europe, most economists (following the lead of political scientists) have conceived the task ahead as one of transition. Transition, however, implies that there is a well-functioning economic norm that should be easy to apply. In the flush of the capitalist "victory" of 1989, economists assumed that market economies would continue to hum along vigorously and facilitate the ready inclusion of the reforming former socialist states. They have since learned that this is not an easy process, at least not in the space of half a decade. Such a lag should not have been surprising, given the time required for stabilization after both world wars. The European states did not re-achieve the Gross National Product levels of 1913 until 1924–25, and it was not until 1949 that they were able to match those of 1938.

As observed above, the waste involved in central planning and the dislocation since 1989 were almost as costly as the physical destruction caused by the wars. Given the two postwar histories, the economic problems of the so-called transition have not been abnormal. Nevertheless, it is far from clear that the difficulties encountered were just a question of underestimating the time required for a successful transition. It is possible that more enduring impediments are involved.

This essay need not recount all the difficulties encountered: the legal and institutional impediments to privatization, the attrition of investment funds, the preoccupation with massive unemployment, and the unwillingness to allow widespread bankruptcies. Janos Kornai has tried to develop a general model to understand the problems that have emerged. Eastern Europe, he suggests, has gone from a sellers' economy, in which purchasers competed for capital and consumer goods, to a buyers' economy in which demand has been slack. Post-Communist economies have dismantled the bureaucratic signals that coordinated economic activity, but they have not yet substituted those of the market. The disastrous collapse of national output has exceeded that of the Great Depression; and although the reasons are not the earlier ones analyzed by John Maynard Keynes, Kornai concedes that some state role to bolster investment may still be necessary. [17]

Perhaps, though, the very concept of transition may prove to be misleading. As Hungarian economist Tamás Réti suggested in his critique of an earlier version of this essay, transition is an ambiguous concept. Part of the difficulty stems from the ambivalence of East European intellectuals and elites. They periodically switch their orientation from West to East and back again, without a decisive commitment. For example, citing G. Enders, Réti described Hungary as a ferryboat that never quite lands on either bank of the river. But there is the even more unsettling question of whether a stable equilibrium for the market economies exists. Where on the Western bank should the ferry land? Again, a comparison with the era after 1919 may be illuminating. Economic historians have argued that the decisive flaw in the interwar economy was its effort to operate on the basis of prewar conditions that could no longer be restored.[18] This thinking was epitomized by the attempted restoration of the gold standard, a mechanism through which central bankers and other policymakers of the 1920s assumed that the great changes wrought by the world conflict would be easily overcome. But in fact, capital had been squandered; the British overseas assets on which the robustness of sterling and ultimately the gold standard rested had been undermined; and the once weak and fragmented working classes, who had already challenged low-wage equilibria between 1910 and 1914, would do so again in the 1920s.

Does the idea of transition play a similar misleading role today by suggesting that the earlier high-performance equilibria of international capitalism remain unchanged, to be achieved by all those who will follow the orthodox rules of the game? Is the world economy not evolving with great rapidity even as the former socialist countries endeavor to find their niche within it? Are Western experts prescribing a model of development that is already badly buffeted? Of course, the recession that gripped the United States and Western Europe until the end of 1993 has made transition in Eastern Europe a far more difficult process. As the economic cycle turns upward and global demand increases, the task of reforming the East European economies may become easier. Still, the hope of a rapid and easy catch-up inherent in the idea of transition may be misplaced.

It is not clear that Western economies will return to the high-employment equilibria that prevailed before the recession of the early 1990s. Even as the service and high-tech sectors in the West generate employment, manufacturing sectors are slow to reemploy their former work force. A new geography of employment and unemployment has emerged, perhaps as a durable feature of the so-called advanced industrial or capitalist states. Large regions in northern Britain, southern Italy, and the urban centers of the United States do not seem capable of generating income or sustaining investment but require continued assistance, whether from their national treasuries or the EU's social funds. Simultaneously, efforts by Western governments to curtail deficits and contain public spending may remove some of the employment possibilities that depressed areas have relied on. In effect, the "Third World" has begun to replicate itself in the lagging regions and city centers of the First. Recovery does not seem likely to eliminate this new geographical division of labor. Is it possible that the former socialist economies will be particularly vulnerable to this global renegotiation of economic roles? If it is unclear how the economic peripheries of North America and the EU will fare in the decades to come, how can we be certain that the economies of Eastern Europe will join the robust poles of development and not stagnate alongside so many other regions? In short, Eastern Europe faces a transition, but to what?

The contradiction that finally undermined the world economy between 1929 and 1931 derived from the triumph of liberal democracy a decade earlier. Wilsonian ideology proposed self-determination on the one hand but a regime of international payments that undermined democracy on the other. With the United States committed to substantial repayment of inter-Allied war loans and Britain and France to reparations, international debt weighed heavily on interest rates. So too did the commitment to revalue or compensate for depreciated paper assets in Britain and Italy, though not in Germany or France. Happily, we have learned something from the interwar period and from the experiences of Latin America in the 1960s and 1970s. Today, as in the interwar period, there has been a race to forgive debts so that democracy can be preserved.

Nonetheless, concessions sometimes come too belatedly to benefit the moderates. Reparations were finally settled in 1932, but too late to keep Hitler from scoring big in elections. (Of course, there were many domestic reasons for Hitler's success, and they may well have been decisive in their own right.) The fate of Russian democracy has likewise seemed in play as Western countries and the International Monetary Fund patch together packages of loans and aid, many of which have been blocked in the pipeline or made conditional upon a monetary stringency that the divided Russian government has proved unable to impose. There are two competing approaches to the contemporary economic turmoil of *l'après-socialisme,* just as there were to the difficulties of *l'après-guerre.* Advocates of rigor argue that the quicker the conversion from wasteful allocations, including wasteful full employment, the better the chances for real wealth and ultimate stability. Advocates of sliding-scale adjustment (and I am not talking of those who want to freeze the status quo) warn that rigor may shatter the political coalitions needed to press forward with privatization, modernization, and democratic entrepreneurship. They propose slowing the tempo of adjustment. Ultimately, economic programs depend on political coalitions and forces. There is now general agreement that the optimal allocation of resources must be based on real prices, on the reduction of subsidies to firms to roughly the level allowed in the West (for the OECD economies certainly retain indirect and direct subsidies!), and on labor mobility. Ironically enough, bankruptcies and firings are becoming the indicator of economic progress. So far, the issue separating policymakers and experts is how best to arrive at a privatized and market economy: with "shock therapy" that may produce a political reaction or with a slower adjustment that may continually postpone confronting economic reality? Market reformers have prevailed in the Czech Republic and generally in Poland but not in the far larger and more complex Russian economy. National-populist coalitions, often led by former Communists, have made political hay by contesting the rigors of reform.

Do the experiences of the interwar economy offer lessons? Only ambiguous ones, as is always the case with history. History cannot dictate whether rigorous reformers in the mold of Václav Klaus are likely to prevail in Russia, or whether we should support "shock therapy" or gradualism. But history should alert us to the possibility that the East European societies may have to make their way in an international economy that is more demanding and challenging than the developmental models their Western tutors have taken for granted. The distribution of haves and have-nots, or at least of regions that generate wealth and those that absorb it, is in rapid flux. Market economies grow stratified in new and intractable ways. Even a successful transition will not ensure uniformly robust economic growth. Interwar economic conditions required breaking the rules of the golden age before World War I. Post-socialist economies will not necessarily become, perhaps no longer can just become, prolongations of the triumphant capitalism of 1989. Both West and East European economies are involved in a transition whose outcome is far from clear. Still, the history of the interwar period should also alert us to the fact that the East and West are mutually dependent; the prosperity of one depends upon the welfare of the other. "Widening" the EU will be difficult; nonetheless, including the former socialist economies remains as urgent a task as completing Western monetary unification. The success of reform will depend on the openness of Western Europe and the United States. Political and economic leaders undermined the vision of 1919 by burdening the international economy with heavy debts, attempting to reimpose a rigid exchange standard, and erecting new tariff walls. Such shortsighted measures should not be allowed to blight the hopes of 1989.

Notes

[1]See, most recently, Rudiger Dornbusch, Wilhelm Nölling, and Richard Layard, eds., *Postwar Economic Reconstruction and Lessons for the East Today* (Cambridge: MIT Press, 1993); and Comité pour l'Histoire Economique et Financière de la France, *Le Plan Marshall et le relèvement économique de l'Europe: Colloque tenu à Bercy les 21, 22, et 23 mars 1991 sous la direction de René Girault et Maurice Lévy Leboyer* (Paris: Ministère de l'Economie des Finances et du Budget, 1993). Discussion of the "contemporary" situation and possible conclusions of the early 1990s.

[2]Teichova, "East-Central and South-East Europe," in Peter Mathias and Sidney Pollard, eds., *Cambridge Economic History of Europe*, 2d ed., vol. 8 (Cambridge: University Press, 1966–89), 897–904.

[3]See Ivan T. Berend, "The Historical Evolution of Eastern Europe as a Region," in Ellen Comisso and Laura D'Andrea Tyson, eds., *Power, Purpose, and Collective Choice: Economic Strategy in Socialist States* (Ithaca: Cornell University Press, 1986), esp. 158–63.

[4]David Mitrany, *The Effect of the War in Southeastern Europe* (New Haven: Yale University Press, 1936), 171.

[5]Teichova, "East-Central and South-East Europe" 8:941–51. For the limits on German successes and domination before Munich, see ibid., 951–56.

[6]In effect, this is Peter Temin's interpretation, *Lessons from the Great Depression* (Cambridge: MIT Press, 1989).

[7]See Charles Kindleberger, *The World in Depression, 1929–1939* (Berkeley and Los Angeles: University of California Press, 1975), and Barry Eichengreen, *Golden Fetters: The Gold Standard and the Great Depression, 1919–1939* (New York: Oxford University Press, 1992).

[8]Teichova, "East-Central and South-East Europe" 8:916–17, 934, 948.

[9]Jochen Bethkenhagen, "RGW und Weltwirtschaft: Konsequenzen zweier wirtschaftskrisen," in Hans-Hermann Hoehmann and Heinrich Vogel, eds., *Osteuropas Wirtschaftsprobleme und die Ost-West-Beziehungen* (Baden Baden: Nomos Verlagsgesellschaft, 1984), 109 (table 3).

[10]See the summary of the different subsidy estimates and methods used to determine them in Vlad Sobel, *The CMEA in Crisis* (New York: Praeger and Center for Strategic and International Studies, 1990), 11–20. See also Michael Marrese, "CMEA: Effective but Cumbersome Political Economy," in Comisso and Tyson, eds., *Power, Purpose, and Collective Choice*, 11–151, for a defense of the Marrese-Vanous calculations. The level of subsidization remains controversial. Of course, oil prices were hardly market prices in any case but were determined by cartel arrangement. For the view that East European economies really bore the economic costs of intrabloc trade, see Laszlo Csaba, *Eastern Europe in the World Economy* (Cambridge: Cambridge University Press, 1990).

[11]For the most convincing recent discussion of the reasons for the Soviet structure of subsidies, see Randall Warren Stone, "Pursuit of Interest: The Politics of Subsidized Trade in the Soviet Bloc" (Ph.D. diss., Harvard University, 1993). Based on extensive internal Russian and East European reports as well as numerous interviews, Stone argues, convincingly I believe, that the development of the Soviet

subsidy cannot be seen as a rational instrument of control over its satellites. Instead, it grew because the system of Soviet central planning led to uncoordinated negotiations and decisions that smaller trade partners could take advantage of; likewise, it could not compensate for world market-price developments.

[12]For an estimate of Hungarian losses after the end of trade subsidies at the beginning of 1991, see Gabor Oblath and David Tarr, "The Terms-of-Trade Effects from the Elimination of State Trading in Soviet-Hungarian Trade," *Journal of Comparative Economics* 16 (1992): 75–93.

[13]See chapter 2 of my forthcoming study *Dissolution: The End of East Germany* (Princeton: Princeton University Press) for a fuller discussion with citations.

[14]The CMEA's intrablock exports dropped from 63.5 percent in 1970 to 55.8 percent in 1982, although CMEA members increasingly sought to reserve their "hard" goods—those that could be traded for Western currencies—for interblock trade while reserving their "soft" goods—those that had no ready Western market—for their bloc partners, including the Soviets, who had to accept such goods in return for oil. See Bethkenhagen, "RGW und Weltwirtschaft," 18–19; see also Laura D'Andrea Tyson, "The Debt Crisis and Adjustment Responses in Eastern Europe: A Comparative Perspective," in Comisso and Tyson, eds., *Power, Purpose, and Collective Choice,* 63–110. She suggests that CMEA exports to the West may in fact have included re-exporting Soviet oil. This was certainly the case for GDR.

[15]"Eastern Europe Survey," *Economist,* 13 March 1993, 9, table 3. The *Economist* offers the consolation that some of this production was of unusable goods and that consumption started to rise even while output fell.

[16]Cited by Janos Kornai, "Transformational Recession: A General Phenomenon Examined through the Example of Hungary's Development" (François Perroux lecture at the College de France, issued as a discussion paper by the Harvard Institute of Economic Research, 1993), 3.

[17]Ibid.

[18]See Temin, *Lessons from the Great Depression,* and Eichengreen, *Golden Fetters.*

Chapter 5

Establishing International Order, Post-1991: Some Lessons of the Yugoslav Crisis

Steven L. Burg

The wars in the former Yugoslavia have made it clear that the principles and practices that provided a stable framework for international security in the era of the cold war are no longer sufficient to preserve peace. The principles of state sovereignty, territorial integrity, human rights, and self-determination embodied in the United Nations Charter and other United Nations (UN) documents as part of the post–World War II attempt to construct an international security framework have proven contradictory (or at least subject to contradictory interpretation) in the wake of the collapse of that framework. National and ethnic actors have appealed to competing principles of international order to legitimate actions that have destabilized states and undermined the stability of interstate relations. The threats that war will spread throughout the Balkans, that fighting will soon engulf the entire Caucasus and its neighbors, and that similar conflicts will erupt elsewhere in the post-Communist world make it urgent to establish a new framework for international security in the post-1991 era, a framework that will be more durable than the one established after 1919.

Much of the instability in the enlarged Europe of the post-1991 era can be attributed to the resurgence of nationalism. Appeals to national identity are central in the legitimation of new states and new governments in the post-1991 era, much as they were in the post-1919 era. Nationalism is a powerful basis on which to elicit popular support when a government cannot as yet generate support based on the improvements it has produced in the material well-being of the population. Nationalist strategies of legitimation are inherently exclusivist in character and reinforce authoritarian tendencies in the domestic politics of new states. The adoption of exclusivist language laws, citizenship laws, or other measures intended to assert the national character of the state or insulate the political power of an ethnic majority against its minority population has stimulated internal conflict between majority and minority populations from the Baltic to the Balkans. The nationalist concept of the state as an instrument for affirming ethnic identity has in some cases led politicians, not all of whom are extremists, to express concern for the well-being of conationals in neighboring states or even to raise demands for redrawing international borders in accordance with ethnic identities. Secessionist and irredentist claims have led to open war in the former Yugoslavia and the Caucasus and threaten to lead to violence elsewhere.

The inherent contradictions among nationalist strategies of legitimation in a world of ethnically heterogeneous states, demands for self-determination that take the form of secessionist movements on the part of national minorities, and traditional definitions of sovereignty and territorial integrity demonstrate the need to develop new understandings of some of the most basic concepts of the international system. At least within the context of the Euro-Atlantic community encompassing North America and Western, Central, and Eastern Europe, it is possible to begin to resolve these contradictions by viewing legitimacy, self-determination, and territorial integrity as claims whose recognition by the international community can be made contingent on evidence of the claimants' commitment to protect human rights and democracy.

The system of sovereign states remains the basic foundation of international stability, but the development of transnational European law and judicial institutions suggests that it may also be useful to consider sovereignty divisible. Secessionist and irredentist issues may in some cases be resolved through shared sovereignty arrangements between neighboring states rather than through the division or transfer of territory between them. At the very least, states cannot be allowed to use their claim to sovereignty to shield their abuse of human rights and democracy and the violent interethnic conflicts they engender from international inquiry.

The dimensions of the challenge inherent in an effort to redefine these concepts are manifest in the development of the Yugoslav crisis.[1] National political leaderships in the West were unable to find principled solutions to conflicts between the heretofore absolute principles called into question by the unfolding crisis. Existing Euro-Atlantic institutions and the UN Security Council system proved inadequate either to avert the outbreak of war or to bring the fighting to a rapid conclusion through negotiation. The mounting human tragedy in Bosnia-Herzegovina revealed the inadequacies of the decision-making principles, operational guidelines, and conflict-management capabilities of Euro-Atlantic institutions such as the Conference on Security and Cooperation in Europe (CSCE), the North Atlantic Treaty Organization (NATO), and the European Union (EU). It also made clear the necessity of expanding UN peacemaking, peacekeeping, and peace-enforcement capacities. At the same time, however, the Yugoslav crisis reaffirmed both the central importance of individual states in defining collective responses to crises and the great difficulties inherent in coordinating divergent national perspectives, policies, and practices. The most obvious weakness, shared by international institutions and individual states alike, was the reactive rather than proactive nature of their efforts.

Evidence that Yugoslavia was disintegrating and that disintegration would lead to violence was clear to academic analysts and midlevel government officials well in advance. But policymakers made few efforts to address the underlying conditions of conflict and to avert the crisis. To become more proactive, Western political leaders will have to broaden the scope of issues that can legitimately be considered of international rather than exclusively domestic concern. The first step in this direction was taken in July 1991 at the CSCE Geneva meeting of experts on national minorities, convened just as war broke out in Slovenia. At that time, the CSCE concluded that issues concerning the rights of minorities "are matters of legitimate international concern and consequently do not constitute exclusively an internal affair of the respective state."[2]

A proactive approach is important in preventing violence, especially in disputes involving competing ethnic claims to the same territory. As the Yugoslav case clearly demonstrates, interethnic violence escalates rapidly and engulfs the civilian population. This narrows the opportunities for outside mediators to reach and implement a negotiated settlement. The onset of violent conflict brings those willing to use violence to the political forefront and pushes nonviolent leaders and groups aside. Advocacy of interethnic accommodation under conditions of violence becomes particularly difficult, both personally and politically. The hostility generated by civilian casualties and the displacement of the civilian population after fighting has broken out make it very difficult for ethnic leaders to extend the kind of mutual concessions usually required to reach a stable settlement.

The Yugoslav experience clearly argues, therefore, for the establishment of an international capacity to help defuse local conflicts before they turn violent and to prevent episodes of interethnic violence from escalating. To defuse conflicts before they turn violent, the international community must consider relations between states and their minorities to be a legitimate subject of international inquiry and must establish mechanisms and practices that can facilitate the resolution of these conflicts. The CSCE's creation of a High Commissioner on National Minorities in July 1992 represents an important step in this direction.[3] But there are few other institutionalized means for resolving either interstate disputes or disputes between states and their minority populations before they turn violent and pose direct threats to international peace.

The Elements of a New Regime

The lack of institutionalized capacities to respond with nonmilitary measures to the threat of escalation inherent in incidents of interethnic violence is a weakness that must be addressed as part of the effort to construct a new framework for international security in the post-1991 era. If future Yugoslav-like wars are to be avoided, nonmilitary means must be devised to respond rapidly and effectively to isolated incidents of interethnic violence, and these must be institutionalized through international organizations. Early involvement by international civilian investigators and judicial personnel in the investigation of incidents of interethnic violence, for example, may prevent manipulation by local extremists. Direct international participation in identifying and penalizing perpetrators of violence can contribute to strengthening local confidence in the fairness of the outcome. Such activities, carried out by civilian personnel and carefully constructed so as to avoid the suggestion of military intervention, may be seen as adaptations of such accepted international practices as monitoring missions. They represent a potentially powerful instrument by which governments can strengthen their domestic and international legitimacy.

The cease-fire in Slovenia in June 1991, the agreement in December 1991 to establish a UN peacekeeping operation in Croatia, and the failure to achieve agreement on a peace plan for Bosnia-Herzegovina before fighting broke out in April 1992 all reflect the fact that local interests rather than international actors determine the success or failure of efforts to settle conflicts through negotiation. The ensuing war in Bosnia-Herzegovina demonstrates not only the extent to which the authority and control of local leaders becomes dissipated under conditions of ethnic war but also the great difficulties of enforcing any agreement that might be reached. It is best, therefore, to engage local leaderships in negotiations before the outbreak of war raises the stakes to a level at which it is difficult for them to make the concessions necessary to achieve a lasting agreement. It is also important not to allow negotiations over ethnic issues to be monopolized by the most extreme parties. Where legitimate representatives of multiethnic or nonethnic forces exist, they should be allowed to play a role in such negotiations. By preventing the escalation of violence, the international community may make it easier to achieve this goal.

In some instances, even early engagement in such issues may be futile as long as the international community refuses to recognize the possibility that the redrawing of borders may constitute one path to a peacefully negotiated solution to an interethnic crisis. In Yugoslavia, for example, secessionist and irredentist claims were advanced by many groups simultaneously. By recognizing that all peoples in a country have equal rights to self-determination, international mediators may be able to lead local actors toward mutual concessions in situations of conflicting claims. The conflicting nature of the claims in Yugoslavia might have provided the basis for mutual concessions had the possibility of redrawing the formerly internal borders been recognized as a means to a resolution. At the very least, those who refused the opportunity to participate in peaceful negotiations to resolve these conflicts could then have been held accountable for their actions from the outset.

Instead of setting the conclusion of a peaceful agreement among all parties as the goal, the United States and other Western nations chose to support the territorial status quo while others opted to support the right of self-determination for the former Yugoslav republics attempting to secede. Both positions reduced the incentives on all sides of the conflict to reach a peaceful agreement and increased the opportunity for local supporters of the status quo to use force against their opponents. Insistence on the status quo failed to prevent the breakup of either the former Soviet Union or Yugoslavia, and insistence on applying the principle of self-determination to boundaries over which there was substantial disagreement contributed to the onset of war.

The situation in Yugoslavia was especially volatile because of the nationalist alliance between Serb leaders in Croatia and Bosnia-Herzegovina and leaders of the Serbian republic and the Yugoslav army. But such cross-border alliances are not exceptional. They are also present, for example, in the Nagorno-Karabakh conflict. Hungarians in Romania and Slovakia and Russians in the Baltic and other former Soviet republics may seek to forge such alliances in the future, especially if more nationalistic governments come to power in Budapest and Moscow. In these cases, as in the case of Yugoslavia, the status of borders imposed by Communist or other authoritarian regimes without popular participation and the rights of ethnic populations established under the policies and politics of the old regime have been called into question. Strong principles other than support for the discredited status quo must be found to settle such questions before they turn violent.

This is not to argue in favor of subordinating principles of territorial integrity and the inviolability of borders to the right of ethnic groups to self-determination. Rather, it is to argue that if the outbreak of violence elsewhere is to be prevented, the international community must affirm the moral and political superiority of principles of human rights and especially of the rule of law over principles of state sovereignty and territorial integrity. Such an affirmation is particularly important in cases of claims to separate statehood based solely on an ethnically defined demand for self-determination. [4] The establishment and protection of individual human rights makes the free expression of linguistic, cultural, and ethnic identities possible. The enforcement of self-determination on the basis of ethnic identity, however, does not guarantee individual freedom. On the contrary, nationalist bases of political legitimation often subordinate the individual to the collective and lead to ethnic exclusivity and political privilege. Human rights should therefore take priority over ethnic self-determination in the resolution of conflict. The international community should not support either authoritarian movements that seek to legitimate their claims to power through appeals to nationalism or democratic nationalist movements that offer no greater democracy than that which has already been established under an existing regime. Democracy, defined as the political order that results from the institutionalization of individual human rights, should be considered superior to ethnic affinity as a basis for sustaining the claims to sovereignty by political regimes.

Similarly, the principle of maintaining territorial integrity should be subordinated to the principle of preserving or advancing democracy. The protection of internationally recognized human rights (not the existence of a coercive central power prepared to enforce existing borders) is the limiting criterion by which secessionist claims should be denied. In this way, the creation of an increasing number of microstates that contribute little to the advance of human rights may be avoided while changes that improve the human condition may be recognized and supported.

The Yugoslav case suggests that by focusing too narrowly on territorial integrity and the preservation of existing borders, external actors may discourage democratic change and inadvertently encourage the use of force. By making peaceful change more difficult, such insistence made violent change more likely. Early attention from outside powers to the democratic legitimation of existing borders might have encouraged newly emergent governments in Croatia and Bosnia to show greater concern for the protection of the human rights of ethnic minorities, thereby avoiding the escalation of ethnic tensions. In such a situation, the importance of articulating—clearly, publicly, and early—the human rights standards against which new governments will be judged cannot be overemphasized. By doing so, international actors may affect popular perceptions and politics. In Yugoslavia, for example, the regional government elected in 1990 in Croatia might have acted more moderately if its human rights policies had been subjected to critical review from the outset.

Bringing multilateral support for human rights and democracy within the Euro-Atlantic community to bear on individual states in this way will require more effective decision-making procedures in the CSCE (now OSCE). As the Yugoslav conflict unfolded, CSCE action was blocked by the opposition of the Yugoslav government, which prevented the establishment of the consensus necessary for action under then-prevailing CSCE rules. The CSCE took the first tentative steps toward correcting this weakness by adopting a "consensus-minus-one" principle of decision making at its Prague meeting in January 1992. It decided that, "in cases of clear, gross, and uncorrected violations of relevant CSCE commitments," appropriate peaceful action to protect human rights, democracy, and the rule of law may be taken, "in the absence of the consent of the State concerned." This action was prompted by the ongoing Yugoslav crisis as well as by concerns that the accession of the post-Soviet republics to CSCE membership made it likely that other, similar situations would arise in the future. Such actions, however, were to be limited to "political declarations or other political steps to apply outside the territory of the State concerned." The Prague meeting avoided authorizing the CSCE to launch more direct activities, such as the dispatch of fact-finding or rapporteur missions, without the prior consent of the state involved. [5]

Conflicts involving competing ethnically legitimated claims to the same territory are among the most difficult to resolve. But the existence of competing claims to territory does not by itself account for the magnitude of human destruction that occurred in Yugoslavia. The extreme violence in this case must also be attributed to the establishment of ethnically defined governments that failed to provide democratic safeguards for the human rights of minority communities. Therefore, if the international community is to facilitate the peaceful settlement of this category of ethnic conflicts, it must devise instruments for preventing ethnic domination and for safeguarding human rights in such territories. The emergence of pooled or even transnational sovereignty in the European Community[6] and especially the development of a European Court for Human Rights to enforce provisions of the European Convention on Human Rights represent possible approaches to the resolution of such conflicts. Sovereignty over a particular population may be shared by neighboring states, and disputes may be resolved by referring them to bi- or multilateral institutions. Thus, Hungary may serve the educational, cultural, or other needs of the ethnically Hungarian population of Romania or Serbia, and Serbia may serve the similar needs of Serbs in Croatia or Bosnia-Herzegovina, while each state retains sovereignty over its own territory.

Such redefinition of principle will not be easy to achieve in practice. The Yugoslav experience provides further evidence that even under conditions of crisis and in a context of high incentives for collective action, leaders of individual states in the Euro-Atlantic community will advocate widely differing and sometimes contradictory responses. International debate over a Western peacekeeping or peacemaking role in Yugoslavia and the creation of the military capacity to play such a role revealed the persistence of conflict between French and American views as well as the great variations among German, British, American, and other European perspectives on intervention in such instances. These differences reflect the pursuit of differing national interests arising out of historical factors, traditional spheres of influence, economic and political ambitions, and even such simple realities as geographic proximity to the country in crisis.

Differences in approach to crisis management also arise out of the differing impact of events on the domestic politics of individual states. By virtue of the presence of large numbers of Croatian and Bosnian *gastarbeiter* in Germany and the firsthand knowledge of Yugoslavia gained by the millions of German tourists who traveled there, the German public was, from the outset, more closely connected to events in Yugoslavia than were the American and other Western publics. This widespread public interest in the issue encouraged the German media to cover events closely and to press the government for action. As a result, from the beginning of 1991, the German government was under greater pressure to act than were other Western governments. By contrast, in the United States, it was not until the summer of 1992 that expanded media coverage of the attack on Sarajevo, widespread coverage of the atrocities committed by Serb forces, and the onset of a presidential election campaign combined to increase domestic pressure for President George Bush to act. In the end, however, no Western leadership was ready to commit its troops to the task of imposing peace in the former Yugoslav republics. Unlike oil-rich Kuwait and Saudi Arabia, the strategic value of the former Yugoslavia and the neighboring Balkan states that might be drawn into an expanded conflict was insufficient to outweigh the domestic political costs of military involvement.

The Yugoslav crisis clearly demonstrated the need to develop a regional capacity for both peacekeeping and peace enforcement. NATO and the Western European Union (WEU) countries acknowledged this in June 1992, when NATO agreed in principle to the possibility of undertaking peacekeeping operations in Eastern Europe if asked to do so by the CSCE and when the WEU countries agreed to the possibility of assigning troops to the WEU for such missions. Under present CSCE rules, however, any request that NATO play such a role would still require a unanimous vote. Individual member states of the WEU retain the authority to make the decision to assign forces to the WEU. Thus, the establishment of a credible capacity for military intervention in support of the principles and policies of the Euro-Atlantic community may continue to be blocked by political differences among individual national leaderships.

The absence of a credible capacity to use force will make peaceful efforts to resolve Yugoslav-like conflicts more difficult. A credible threat that force might eventually be used against them is often the only means by which to persuade the participants in severe ethnic conflicts to engage in peaceful efforts to resolve their differences and to convince parties threatened by superior force that they will not be further victimized in a post-settlement environment. Key participants in the negotiations carried out under the aegis of the International Conference on the Former Yugoslavia in Geneva have suggested privately that the absence of a credible international commitment to enforce a settlement undermined their ability to settle the Bosnian war in late 1992. The public record of developments in early 1993 reinforces that conclusion.[7] But neither proactive political measures nor reactive military involvement alone can establish the basis for lasting solutions to such conflicts. The contrast between developments in Europe after 1919 and developments after 1945 suggests that lasting solutions to intergroup violence are to be found instead in the web of common material interests arising out of economic integration and in the consolidation of stable democratic regimes in the post-Communist states.

Notes

[1]For a more complete account, see Steven L. Burg, "The International Community and the Yugoslav Crisis," in Milton Esman and Shibley Telhami, eds., *International Organizations and Ethnic Conflict* (Ithaca: Cornell University Press, 1995), 235–271.

[2]*Report of the CSCE Meeting of Experts on National Minorities* (Geneva, 1991), art. II, par. 3.

[3]Conference on Security and Cooperation in Europe, *CSCE's High Commissioner on National Minorities* (Washington, D.C., June 1993).

[4]Steven L. Burg, "Avoiding Ethnic War: Lessons of the Yugoslav Crisis," *Twentieth Century Fund Newsletter* 2, no. 2 (Fall 1992): 1, 4, 11.

[5]Conference on Security and Cooperation in Europe, *Prague Document on Further Development of CSCE Institutions and Structures* (30 January 1992), par. 16, 22.

[6]See Robert O. Keohane and Stanley Hoffmann, "Institutional Change in Europe in the 1980s," and Wolfgang Wessels, "The EC Council: The Community's Decisionmaking Center," in Robert O. Keohane and Stanley Hoffmann, eds., *The New European Community* (Boulder, Colo.: Westview, 1991), 1–39, 133–54.

[7]Steven L. Burg and Paul S. Shoup, *Ethnic Conflict and Geopolitics in the Balkans: A Workshop on Peace in Bosnia Herzegovina* (Washington, D.C.: International Research and Exchanges Board and the Woodrow Wilson International Center for Scholars, 1993).

Chapter 6

Collective Security: 1919 and Now

David N. Dilks

> *The members of the League undertake to respect and preserve*
> *as against external aggression the territorial integrity and ex-*
> *isting political independence of all Members of the League. In*
> *case of any such aggression or in cases of any threat or danger*
> *of such aggression, the Council shall advise upon the means by*
> *which this obligation shall be fulfilled.*
> Article X of the Covenant of the League of Nations

The League of Nations Covenant also stated that any member of the League of Nations resorting to war in disregard of its obligations under earlier articles should be deemed to have committed an act of war against all other members, an action that would immediately cut off trade and financial relations. The Council would advise what military strength the members should contribute to the armed forces that would be used to protect the covenants of the League. In U.S. President Woodrow Wilson's conception, peace would henceforward rest on "a force . . . so much greater than the force of any nation . . . or any alliance hitherto formed or projected that no nation . . . no probable combination of nations could face or withstand it." But there was another essential part of Wilson's framework: that national armaments should be reduced "to the lowest point consistent with domestic safety." This needs to be read with the last of his principles, given in his address to Congress on 8 January 1918: "A general association of nations must be formed under specific covenants for the purpose of affording mutual guarantees of political independence and territorial integrity to great and small states alike." Informed that Wilson had proclaimed fourteen points, the French premier Georges Clemenceau merely observed,[1] "Même le bon Dieu n'avait besoin que de dix" ("Even the good Lord needed only ten").

The conception of collective security was not a new one. It has long held its attractions for international lawyers and political scientists. It was written into the Covenant, as was a good deal else, on the assumption that the United States would be an active and willing partner in the new arrangements. The very fact that it had worldwide application, at least on paper, increased its theoretical attractions and diminished its practical possibilities. The League was left with a largely European membership, since the United States played no part and Japan little. On the face of it, the argument seemed simple enough. The balance of power had failed for the paradoxical reason that the balance itself had proved too even. Despite colossal efforts on the part of all the European protagonists, the victorious side had prevailed only at a cost in life and treasure so high as to be previously unimaginable. Was it not obvious that for a system that had failed so grotesquely, something should be substituted that would provide openness instead of secrecy, procedure instead of improvisation, informed discussion to replace suspicion, deliberation by contrast with the fearful and fumbling reactions of July 1914, and an end to the arms race supposed by many to have been itself a cause of war?

In sum, the purpose of the new system was to create a different kind of balance—an imbalance so plain that no state would dare to challenge it because the likelihood of success would be so small and the prospect of condemnation so obvious. In fact, there were more similarities between collective security and the old balance of power than the enthusiasts for the former would have cared to concede. Each system depended on deterrents and, as a last resort, on the will to fight.[2]

The victorious Allies could hardly turn their backs on nationalism or doubt that it was the coming force. Each had appealed time and again and in the most dire circumstances to patriotic feelings in its own country. Each had felt the effect of

Germany's national pride, discipline, and martial prowess. None felt the least enthusiasm for trying conclusions with Germany again, which explains much about the interwar years. As the British statesman Winston Churchill used to remark with pardonable exaggeration, it had taken half the world more than four years to bring Germany down. To exalt the notion of nationhood was thus natural and inevitable in the peacemaking after World War I. After all, was that not the dominant trend and lesson of the nineteenth century? How else to explain the unification of Italy and Germany? Did not the demise of the Austro-Hungarian and Turkish Empires demonstrate the moral afresh? Had not the Allies themselves exploited this fact to hasten the downfall of the Habsburgs by promising that new states based on defensible national boundaries would replace the rotting structures of the old empire? And did not the British, with their recognition that the Dominions must govern themselves and take separate places on the international stage, believe that they had discovered the secret of combining empire with liberty?

The statesmen of 1919 consciously tried to catch the hoofbeat of the horse of history. Some were no doubt more cynical, and some more realistic, than others. Plainly, the organization of a League based on collective security would become more problematic as the number of nations increased. Lord Curzon, foreign secretary in Britain from 1919 to 1924, once remarked—with a sigh—that whatever else might be said for the League, international life had been a great deal less complicated after the settlement of 1815, when the representatives of four or five Great Powers could settle the fate of Europe. But, as he acknowledged, they could do that only if they agreed on the great matters, and the fate of the Concert of Europe, revived from time to time in the nineteenth century, did not inspire confidence. Moreover, to adopt as nearly as might be the principle of nationality as the basis of the new arrangements for the frontiers of Europe might reduce the need for collective security (or rather, for expensive sacrifices in defense of it) by removing a principal cause of war. Did that not seem to be the lesson of the Near Eastern and Balkan crises that had occurred with regularity before 1914? After 1919 the Great Powers either lacked sufficient identity of interests or did not see any such identity. The purpose of the French was to reinsure themselves against German resurgence and to make the League essentially a vehicle for French interests. Collective security of a limited kind was for France an interest of the first order. French interests required the League to stand foursquare by the settlement of 1919. So long as it was observed, France could not be threatened in a serious way by Germany. Moreover, France was the most important patron of the states created, re-created, or reshaped by the settlement—Poland, Czechoslovakia, Yugoslavia, and Romania. The British had different preoccupations. Europe was the only continent on which they did not have territory to defend. Through the empire, they were in effect trying to operate a system of collective security of their own and on no mean scale. Their large navy and more modest army had been essentially intended to defend the sea routes and bring succor to imperial interests, whether threatened from within, as during the Boer War, or from without. Hence the defense of India formed a predominant point of British military thinking at least until 1907.

Had the United States played a strong role in the League, worldwide collective security still might not have been achieved, but the system might have been more effective in some areas. Whether the Japanese would have been willing to challenge openly a League in which the United States took a prominent part is at least open to debate. Had the French possessed, as they believed they did when the treaty was signed in 1919, an Anglo-American guarantee of their frontiers, French behavior toward Germany might have been different. Indeed, as a guarantor, the United States would have been in a position to press France strongly in that matter, but only on condition that the United States could provide tangible guarantees of security.

With the defeat of Germany and Austria-Hungary, the cement of the victorious coalition crumbled, just as it had done with the collapse of Napoleon Bonaparte in 1815 and would do again with the surrender of Germany in 1945. In 1919 no other great enemy, actual or potential, seemed to be in sight. Despite stern demands on China during the war, Japan appeared to abate its claims and remained allied with the British until 1922. This alliance was abandoned by the British with much regret, partly because of pressure from the United States and Canada.

Collective Security and Collective Defense

After 1945 the story was different. The role of the United States in World War II, both in Europe and in the Far East, was vastly greater than in World War I. Western and Central Europe lay exhausted, starved, ruined. But Russia immediately loomed up as a hostile, suspicious power, apparently capable of trampling across the western part of the continent. As Churchill mused one night in 10 Downing Street a few months before the war's end, "What will lie between the white snows of Russia and the white cliffs of Dover?"[3] Partly because of Joseph Stalin's own squandering of others' goodwill, partly because the powers of Western Europe (especially Britain and France) showed sufficient nerve to do something for themselves, and most of all because the United States took a new view of its responsibilities, collective security of a limited but vital kind became a possibility in the shape of the North Atlantic Treaty Organization (NATO).

It is characteristic of each generation to imagine that the challenges confronting it are somehow greater or more fearful than those of the past. In Europe that would be a view hard to sustain, so cataclysmic have been the events of this century. A work just published in Russian, *Grif Sekretnosti Snyat* (*The Secret Stamp Removed*), indicates that in a span of seventy years, beginning at the end of World War I, the Soviet Union lost nearly 10 million men and women in action. Over 29 million others are recorded to have been wounded, ill, or stricken with frostbite. The war between Russia and Germany from 1941 to 1945 cost 8.66 million killed and missing. The Red Army lost nearly 1 million men, dead and missing, in the civil war of 1918–22, and more than 6 million were wounded in the same period. The war with Finland, lasting no more than a few months in the winter of 1939–40, brought losses of 126,075 killed and missing and 264,900 wounded. Even these staggering figures represent only part of the truth because to assess the price to Soviet Russia, we need to take into account civilian losses, whether from death in concentration camps or by disease, emigration, and the natural loss resulting from a fall in the birthrate. There were more than 5 million Soviet prisoners in World War II. Fewer than 2 million returned. In other words, some 3 million were shot, starved, or beaten to death.[4]

As has been persuasively argued, we should perhaps relabel the collective security embodied by NATO as "collective defense."[5] The distinction on this reading is that collective security has neither predetermined coalitions nor predetermined enemies and that the purpose of such security is the general one of defending the existing order against violent change. By contrast, for more than forty years, NATO was sustained as an alliance against the Soviet Union and its allies. NATO embodied collective defense in the sense that an attack on one member was to be treated as an attack on all, but with significant qualifications. The geographical scope of the commitment was limited. The United States insisted on a qualifying clause about the obligation to go to war, and in practice, the ability of other states to fight might have been constrained by the circumstances of the moment. That said, it was the massive presence of the United States in Europe and the sheer weight of its economy and technological strength that made the alliance credible.

We now witness a situation that would have seemed inconceivable even a few years ago. Some of the states of Eastern Europe have applied to join an alliance the original purpose of which was to deter them and their Russian overlords. So great is the transformation in the world's affairs that NATO itself was able to hold a conference in Budapest in early June 1993. There Hungarian Foreign Minister Geza Jeszenszky remarked that although the danger of large military conflicts had receded, the East-Central European nations (as he termed them) were feeling far from safe. There was no structure of cooperation in security that could respond to the challenges of today's transition to the market-based economy. Jeszenszky remarked that the politicians of Western Europe had been unprepared for the changes in East-Central Europe and that the existing structure of security was capable of handling neither the conflicts that had already erupted nor those still latent. He expressed the belief that in the near future the new democracies would need to establish, jointly with the Western democracies, a system of security that would work. "It is the strategic aim of Hungary . . . to integrate into the Euro-Atlantic system of institutions in politics, legislation, economy, security, and defense." At the same meeting, Prime Minister József Antall of Hungary provided what the founders of the alliance would have regarded as a powerful vindication of their judgment and policies. He called NATO the most important stabilizing factor, both politically and militarily, in Europe. He asked the West for a consistent regional policy, especially regarding the crisis of the former Yugoslavia. In his view, Western leaders should also consider the fragility of the political equilibrium, and the NATO powers should ask themselves how much the nations of Eastern and Central Europe can bear. Ethnic problems might lead to further conflicts in the region, and the leaders of NATO should think about prevention of as well as reaction to crises.[6]

To be sure, NATO has recently offered its resources to the Conference on Security and Cooperation in Europe (CSCE) for peacekeeping operations on that continent and has also made a similar offer to the United Nations (UN) itself. Forces from NATO and the Western European Union (WEU) are playing a part, albeit a limited one, in the present turmoil in the former Yugoslavia. The CSCE and the WEU have roles larger than anyone would have predicted for them a year or two ago. Nevertheless, neither has the structure or underpinning to provide security against a major threat.

When Anthony Eden, the first British minister to pay an official visit to Stalin's Russia, took lunch with the foreign minister near Moscow in 1935, his party found stamped on the butter the words "Peace is indivisible."[7] There is a fine irony about the time and place, of course; but if we look forward twenty or thirty years to the era when two Great Powers jostled for mastery, the notion was not entirely a foolish one. Over a good part of the globe, there was a real risk that peace would indeed prove indivisible, in the sense that a trial of strength almost anywhere, from Northern Europe to the Adriatic or the Black Sea to the easternmost reaches of Russia's empire, might bring the two great protagonists into positions from which they could not withdraw. Nor was the danger confined to direct clashes between the two. We recall more easily the confrontation over Cuba in 1962 than the crises over Formosa or U.S. Secretary of State John Foster Dulles's consideration of the use of atomic weapons in Indochina in 1954. That said, collective security or collective defense in the forty years from the creation of the UN did not apply all over the world. On the contrary, its essential embodiment in the shape of NATO had strictly defined spheres of action. The policymakers during those four decades had to face perils less widely dispersed than those of the 1930s. Italy was no longer a threat, nor was Japan. The United States, by virtue of its strength and willingness to make sacrifices and to place a large army in Europe, occupied a stronger position than any power had occupied in the League between the wars.

Raymond G. H. Seitz, then U.S. ambassador in London, stated in 1992 that the Clinton administration would continue to pursue the broad interests that have governed American policies in

Europe since World War I. The sinews of the policy would be these: to spare no effort to secure political and economic change in Eastern Europe, because a Europe democratic only in part would be a dangerous Europe; to support the process of European integration, but with no particular formula or timetable and not regarding the European Community as the exclusive instrument ("We should be dismayed," he said, "by a Europe sliding back to the days of 'competing nationalisms,'" but at least part of Europe would seem to fit that description only too tidily at the moment); to play an active part in the affairs of Europe with a continuing military presence; and to support reform in the republics of the former Soviet Union, particularly Russia. "If reform there fails, a dark shadow will again be thrown across our world." The most sanguine observer, however, could hardly claim that the outlook in that respect has improved since the ambassador made his statement at the end of 1992. At the same time, Seitz stressed that the American agenda stretches far beyond Europe and that Europeans must appreciate that the United States is equally a Pacific power. Nor is that agenda to be defined only in terms of a political stability depending on military strength. As President Bill Clinton has indicated, traditional conceptions of security will have to be redefined. The economic element must bulk larger.[8] Just as diplomacy is in wartime the twin of strategy, so security in time of peace must be sought through trade and economic coordination, as well as by the possession of armed strength.

No more than President Wilson are we immune from an uncomfortable, often lethal, combination of facts. The distribution of national groups does not fit with political borders in many places, and for all the talk about nationalism as outmoded, passions based on a shared race or language, or on detestation of an enemy or rival, beat more persistently than ever. All this is as true outside Europe as within. In mid-March 1993 explosions in Bombay killed two hundred people and injured a thousand more. The first reaction of some spokesmen was to blame "India's persistent enemies," meaning Pakistan. Simultaneously, it was suggested that the responsibility might lie with the Tamil Tigers fighting in northern Sri Lanka. And all this, we may observe, happened in an area where the British in their imperial phase produced a result that would otherwise have seemed incredible—political unification for a great deal of the Indian subcontinent, a region as large as Europe. The British had struggled

hard until a late date to embrace the whole area in a federal solution that would have included the present-day Bangladesh and
Pakistan. The same purpose was seen in other parts of the former British Empire. The huge state of Nigeria resembles nothing
that went before and has been held together only at the cost of
a murderous civil war and increased delegation of powers from
the center. The dilemma of the British resembled that of other
imperial powers in Africa and Asia. In most instances, they
found no settled boundaries or coherent administrative systems.
They left behind them much larger units, sometimes with
boundaries drawn in the wrong places—"wrong" because the
boundaries cut across tribal divisions. But even where nature has
drawn the boundaries, the problems still prevail. We may think
of Cyprus, where the British expended much money and political credit in resisting not the usual and understood cry for freedom from British rule, but a claim for a union with Greece that
would plainly never be accepted by the substantial Turkish minority. There the apparent requirements of collective defense, as
expressed through the structures of NATO and the Central
Treaty Organization (CENTO), clashed with another principle.
Even when the demand for the union with Greece was abandoned and independence for Cyprus substituted, the day of
reckoning between the Turkish and the Greek interests could not
be postponed indefinitely.

For more than forty years after World War II, Russian behavior posed some of the same dilemmas for the Western powers
that German policy had posed under Adolf Hitler. All critical
opinion was suppressed. There were no awkward elections to
worry about. There was no parliament that might throw out the
government. No old-fashioned notions about the rights of other
powers obtruded. Every technique of propaganda and outright
deceit was employed. As Britain's permanent representative at
the UN remarked to Churchill during the renewed rape of
Czechoslovakia in 1948: "What forces itself on one's attention is
the degree to which everything favours the evil-doer, if he is bla-
tant enough. Any honest Government fights (in peace time) with
two hands tied behind its back. The brilliant blatancy of the Russians is something we can admire but cannot emulate. It gives
them a great advantage."[9]

In the last oration of his public life, Churchill observed that
the world was divided intellectually and to a large extent geo-
graphically between the creeds of Communist discipline and of

individual freedom. He described this as a period "happily unique in human history" and spoke of antagonisms as deep as those that had led to the Thirty Years' War. Force and science, hitherto the servants of man, threatened to become his master. Explaining why Britain had decided to make the hydrogen bomb, Churchill added that safety could lie only in deterrence. The very power of the weapons now available to man might enable the nations at last to live in peace: "Then it may well be that we shall by a process of sublime irony have reached a stage in this story where safety will be the sturdy child of terror, and survival the twin brother of annihilation."[10]

During this period of deep fear of Russia, the leaders of all the NATO powers were conscious of a paradox: they might preserve the peace only if they could show by some means or other that they were willing to fight. Governments depending on re-election found it no easy business to sustain military spending at a high pitch. It is arguable that the enormous military budget of the United States during the 1980s helped to bring the cold war to its end. The stakes had been raised to a level that Russia could match neither in technology nor in cash. But the issue is more complicated than that.

The nature of nuclear warfare rules out old conceptions of collective security as defined in 1919 or even after 1945: patient examination of the facts, an opportunity for passions to cool, sanctions by orderly stages. Only a group of powers organized long in advance and committing great resources over many years could hope to utter a credible threat against a power with nuclear weapons or fight a war against it. That does not mean that some form of collective defense could not apply against lesser powers. It would not be beyond the physical strength of NATO and WEU, if they were so minded, to enforce their will in the former Yugoslavia. Whether the interests at stake for them would justify the risk is another matter. It is customary to say in such instances (the failure to apply effective sanctions to Italy in 1935–36 being the most commonly cited case) that it was not in the interests of the powers that could act to do anything decisive. The point is more accurately put by saying that the cost of taking action seemed to be outweighed by considerations of national interest. In other words, even a limited form of collective security can work only if a sufficient number of states are convinced that the preservation of international order through the containment of an aggressor is in itself a major national interest.

This is a conviction that depends much on a view of history. It is hard to believe, for example, that a good tally of nations would have risked what they did in Korea in 1950 and after had they not been conscious of events of the 1930s.

It is said that although history does not repeat itself, historians repeat themselves. The two most obvious differences between the situation of 1919 and that of 1993 are that Germany is not a defeated and embittered power and that the United States plays a large part in international affairs, indeed a larger part by far than any other power. NATO, whatever its frailties, remains the agency through which the United States and Canada continue to be involved in the security of Europe; hence the significance of the Hungarian foreign minister's insistence that Hungary's strategic aim is to integrate into the "Euro-Atlantic system of institutions." Now that military alliances loom, at least for the moment, less largely than they have done since World War II, it is easy to forget these distinctions and almost to conflate NATO and the European Union (EU) in our thinking. But NATO includes the United States and Canada and does not, for all its functions, include France, whereas the EU naturally excludes the United States and, for good measure, a large part of historic Europe. Much of NATO's strength has lain in the fact that for forty years it has enabled the growing strength of Germany to be harnessed in a way acceptable to the other Western powers. The present confusion in Russia makes it difficult to predict the future. Although the members of the EU committed themselves at Maastricht to the adoption of a common foreign and security policy, there is little sign of it in the former Yugoslavia or elsewhere.

And are we not in the presence of a change in the nature of power as exercised among the states, a change that goes far beyond a reshuffling of alliances or an increase in fluidity? No doubt for mingled and varying reasons, governments are deliberately divesting themselves of powers previously thought indispensable or highly desirable. That is the meaning of the programs of privatization being practiced with vigor in countries all over Europe. To control the commanding heights of the economy used to be the ambition of many governments, democratic as well as tyrannical. Insistence that such powers were the indispensable basis of the state's ability to regulate its own economy underlay many of the objections of Britain's postwar Labour government to the proposals for a European coal and steel community. Now many governments have abandoned exchange controls and have seen no inconsistency between that policy and a determination to maintain values for their currencies fixed within narrow limits. Governments stake not only huge sums of money but also their political credit on the maintenance of their currency at a particular value, only to discover that no defense left to them will enable the dike to be held. In the new circumstances, the pressure that can be brought to bear against a weakened currency is greater than any government or banking system seems able to withstand.

The events of September 1992, when the pound exited the Exchange Rate Mechanism, the devaluation of many of the EU currencies since then, and the reported loss of all of France's foreign exchange reserves in the futile attempt to defend the franc at its old parity in July 1993 all give painful point to the new circumstances. The flow of information can no longer be controlled, a fact that played a substantial part in the undermining of the post–World War II Soviet Empire. Applied science enables more goods to be produced by fewer pairs of hands, but the capacity of economies to create new employment lags well behind those gains of productivity and the international effects of heavy indebtedness. To put the point in a different way, the possession of great resources in terms of population, military strength, or territory does not necessarily bring matching power on the international stage. The collapse of the Soviet Union is but a spectacular example of the powerful currents running just below the surface of international affairs. In these new circumstances, military strength and economic power are not as directly connected as they once were. Nor is military power required to ensure economic success. On the contrary, Japan's example over the last forty years and that of other countries in Southeast Asia in the last twenty years might be held to show that the development of a robust economy is aided by a lack of military strength and the heavy spending that inevitably accompanies it, provided that fortunate circumstances or other powers will guarantee security against attack.[11]

The Limits of European Union

In 1993, after bitter experiences and many failures, we expect less than our grandparents did. We do not have to be unduly skeptical to disbelieve most of the present rhetoric about European monetary union or, still more, political union. It is not only in Britain that a chasm has opened between the protestation of governments on the one hand and doubting public opinion, spread across all political parties, on the other. On all the present evidence, the profound political antagonisms and uncertainties in Germany would be sufficient by themselves to prevent any early realization of the spacious plans of recent times. U.S. policy has been to encourage the unification of Europe. But the EU shows many signs of outright hostility to the United States, and the position of the British is one of peculiar delicacy. Britain's trade with the United States is large and its investment there enormous. Like the rest of Europe, Britain remains heavily dependent on American armed strength. The collapse, for the time being, of the Russian military threat poses problems different from those caused by the collapse of Germany in 1918 because the removal of Russia's hand from much of Central and Eastern Europe did not derive from military defeat. Nor is Russia occupied and disarmed, as Germany was for a time after 1919 and 1945. Hatreds of a kind difficult to imagine in more peaceable places occupy our attention and bewilder our senses every day in the former Yugoslavia and in parts of the old Soviet Empire.

President Boris Yeltsin has asked that Russia be entrusted with the task of keeping peace in the erstwhile Soviet Union. This would be collective security, but of a kind imposed and desired by the imperial power. He points out that Russia possesses "a heartfelt interest in stopping all armed conflicts on the territory of the former Soviet Union."[12] Whether even Russia could impose a peace by force over areas so vast and rebellious is open to doubt, particularly with the chronic economic instability and loss of confidence visible in Moscow. Even if the world were willing to grant the permission that Yeltsin seeks, or if he awarded it to himself, such an ambition would require the capacity to intervene in theaters separated by thousands of miles, from the Baltic States to Central Asia, from Moldova to Tajikistan, from Georgia and Armenia to Azerbaijan and the regions bordering on Afghanistan. Russia's advance across those regions in the nineteenth century aroused deep fear among the British because Russia had a vast army and they did not. The greater the turmoil, the greater the disincentive to bring the countries of the old Soviet Empire into the full ambit of NATO. The game would not be seen to be worth the candle—that is, the likely benefits would not be commensurate with the obvious increase in risk.

Operation Desert Storm provided an example of a limited col-

lective security working in peculiar circumstances. The cause itself was hardly heroic, though Iraqi aggression against Kuwait
could not have been more plainly demonstrated. But the transformation in the Russian position drastically altered the picture
in a matter of months. The new Russia was willing to collabo-
rate with the United States and, to a lesser degree, with Britain
and the other powers that joined the temporary coalition. There
are some parallels with the UN's action over Korea in 1950. In
each war, the United States supplied the bulk of the forces. In
each instance, the UN could play a substantial role because the
use of the veto was not to be feared. In 1950 the Soviet Union
walked out of the Security Council; in 1991 the Russian government in effect forswore its former policies. When the initial decisions were made, neither case seemed likely to involve
campaigning on a grand scale or the use of atomic or nuclear
weapons. Even in 1991, however, to imagine that a limited and
successful operation in the Middle East would herald a new international order required a triumph of hope over experience.
Such an order would entail at least the reduction of military
forces to the lowest point adequate for national defense, an
agreement that changes in international boundaries or jurisdic-
tions would be accomplished only by legitimate methods of consent, the reduction of nuclear weaponry to modest levels,
generally free access to markets, and the observance of accepted
standards of human rights.[13] To count on a new world order
would be premature even in more tranquil times. The British
economist John Maynard Keynes used to say, not entirely in mis-
chief, "In politics it is the unexpected which happens, always."
The same dictum applies to international affairs. Some thirty
years ago, the British foreign secretary asked the chief of the defense staff how many armed conflicts Britain had engaged in
since 1945 and how many of them had been accurately foreseen.
He received the crisp reply, "Forty-eight and none."[14]

The only thing completely unpredictable about the former Soviet Union, allege the wits, is its past, the official version of
which has been adjusted so frequently that those following the
line have performed more contortions in recent times than they
might care to count. In his speech to the Houses of Parliament
in London on the eve of Armistice Day 1992, President Yeltsin
invited the Western nations to join Russia in a new democratic
alliance with common values and common enemies, among
which he named Iraq. He stated that Churchill had been right to

regard the former Soviet Union as a Communist aggressor and (with a perhaps unconscious echo of Franklin Delano Roosevelt) also said that the policy of quarantine had been proved right by time. He went on to say that the new democratic Russia had cast aside the "lies, duplicity, and terror" of the old regime. Discussing the danger of another attempted coup in Russia, he told the world that the ghosts of the past would not triumph.[15] This was a proposition on which no sensible government would bank for some time to come.

We should dismiss from our minds any talk about "the end of history," a phrase that is a contradiction in terms unless we assume a cataclysm so great that the population of the earth is obliterated. We have only to think how rapidly the situation has changed, and for the worse, since 1992. In the year or two before that, the countries behind the former Iron Curtain had regained at least some of their freedoms. The Soviet Empire was disintegrating almost daily. The Red Army was retreating to its heartland. The wall in Berlin had fallen amid jubilation. The prospect of a nuclear war seemed suddenly remote or impossible. The Russians recognized that their campaign in Afghanistan had been as unfruitful as, and more prolonged than, those of the British in earlier times. Kuwait had been successfully defended and Iraq humbled. Not for two hundred years, since the early phase of the French Revolution, had such momentous changes taken place, except as the consequence of a major war.

It would be an intrusion on public grief to mock unduly the high hopes of a short while ago. To adapt the words of an Elizabethan dramatist, the present story is one too sad to insist on. The uncertain economic circumstances of some countries and the dire plight of many; the widespread disenchantment with political institutions; the chaotic condition of Russia, a power still possessing many deadly weapons and enormous armed forces; the tribal hatreds and wanton cruelty in the former Yugoslavia; ancestral voices prophesying war and, worse still, countless people engaged in open or undeclared war not only in the old Soviet Union but also in South America, many parts of Africa, and some parts of Asia; the protestation that nations are moving toward larger aggregations and the subordination of the nation-state at the very moment when groups (sometimes of no more than a few million or even less) are claiming separate status—all this means, at the least, a prolonged period of instability, requiring high levels of statesmanship, patience, and long-term views. To take no other example, how is international security to be viewed against the probability that within a few years, nuclear weapons will be in the hands of a number of small- or middle-rank powers?

An optimist would reply that conditions are so transformed that some of the major obstacles of the past have vanished or diminished and would cite the greater commitment to democracy, the free flow of information, the new patterns of economic activity, and a greater sense of interdependence among states.[16] Those very facts, however, remind us that security cannot be considered only in the context of Europe. Even where the European powers have made a conscious effort to adjust boundaries, the results have often been unhappy to a desperate degree. That is true, for instance, in Somalia and the Sudan. Examples of a different kind might be sought in the Middle East (the West Bank, Lebanon, Syria), in Yugoslavia, and in Iraq itself. It is no doubt highly unfashionable to point out that the European empires attempted to provide security, in the case of the British on a very large scale. It was understood that a serious attack on any part of the empire would be resisted by all parts. That at least was the theory, and although Britain was not attacked directly in 1914 or 1939, she was sustained not only by the dependent territories, which—it may well be argued—had no choice, but also by the Dominions, which certainly had. It was accepted in the 1930s that if the Japanese assaulted Singapore or, less plausibly, Australia and New Zealand, or cut the trade routes, Britain would be required to go to war at the other end of the world, however great the dangers in Europe. Only the fear of being overwhelmed by Germany caused that pledge to be qualified in 1939. Inadequate though this kind of collective security may have been, it was nevertheless a good deal more than has been provided by most other methods during the twentieth century. The European empires considered it their duty to maintain a respectable administration and to suppress internal disorder. The slaughter, genocide, starvation, and corruption that have afflicted Zaire, Uganda, the Sudan, and Somalia, to look no further, are worse than anything that occurred under the imperial rule of the British or the Belgians. There is more than a little irony in the presence of a substantial U.S. force in Somalia. After all, no other government more persistently condemned the evils of colonialism than that of the United States, and because the United States was central to the defense of all the West European powers, that condemnation carried weight. It remains to be seen whether the United States will follow the only course that could enable it to carry out the stated purposes of its mission in Somalia—that is, to practice imperialism and set up what would amount to a colonial administration.

The role of the UN has grown. The fact that it manifestly lacks the strength to provide physical security against a Great Power does not mean that it can do nothing for security in other senses. The British foreign secretary, recently remarking that the UN has the unique legal authority to maintain international peace and security, prudently added that the expectations of its ability to fulfill this role stand perhaps too high: "Dr. Boutros-Ghali sits on the thirty-eighth floor of the UN, whence he is expected to run a Foreign Ministry, a Defence Ministry, and a World Ministry of Development Planning. The international community asks him to take on these tasks, but fails to give him the resources he needs." Even in these days of reduced forces, the British have 80,000 troops in service abroad and a further 20,000 in Northern Ireland. Of the former total, some 4,000 are at the disposal of the UN in Kuwait, Cyprus, Cambodia, the former Yugoslavia, Somalia, and the Western Sahara. France has about 6,000 troops serving the UN in similar missions.[17]

According to recent forecasts, the population of the world will rise by about half in one generation. Almost all those extra mouths will have to be fed in the so-called Third World. In the advanced countries, the population will in some instances creep upward (mainly because of increased longevity) and in other instances stabilize or decline. The fact that apocalyptic forecasts have been put forward before and have been proved wrong should not make us indifferent to these prospects. Is it conceivable that such a vastly increased population could even subsist without inflicting irreversible biological damage to the earth? If so, how? How can so great a number of people be fed? Will states with teeming populations tolerate growing disparities of wealth and immigration policies designed to keep populations stable? Instead of anxiously awaiting reports of Szczecin (Stettin) and Trieste, or of the North-West Frontier and the Mekong Delta, shall we in twenty years' time be nervously scanning the news of warfare in Africa and South Asia? Shall we in Europe and North America not have to think of "security" in broader terms, on practical and moral grounds alike?

An Unstable Balance of Power?

Much depends on the trading and political relations between the powers and on their forms of government. If democratic states can be built or rebuilt from the wreckage of the Communist bloc, there may be hope. Only the most sanguine would believe that the process could be quick or sure. It has been shown that the relationship between this process and collective security is close because the latter is a transfer, to the international level, of a domestic system that is used by democracies to resolve conflicts and that relies on the rule of law within and between nations and on a commitment to resolve disputes peacefully. All parties have to accept the legitimacy of the formula for resolving disputes. In this view, the build up of collective security in the new Europe will depend on the creation of stable democracies that share a broadly similar approach. Until that time comes, Europe must make do with a hybrid system. A strong Western alliance will be needed in conjunction with a limited arrangement for collective security under the CSCE.[18] It is probable that, in the absence of a clear threat from a great power, collective security or defense will remain an aspiration unless its form and scope are limited. The Wilsonian view, based on a reading of the origins of World War I, called for the rejection of exclusive or entangling alliances. Yet, if NATO is an example of collective defense that has worked, this is because NATO was an enlarged alliance confronting an obvious enemy, possessing political will and the support of the strongest power.

In the speech already quoted, Ambassador Seitz remarked that the world of the new century (and he might have given a date earlier than that) may turn out to be one that is more familiar to the practiced historian than to the casual observer. In place of a world organized around two superpowers, we may see nation-states jockeying for individual advantage, with the weak cowering and the strong strutting, "a world of bluster and platitudes where there is no penalty and no reward because we are busy with our own narrow pursuits and look about inattentively or indifferently." This he described as a balance-of-power world, one without inspiration or moral dimension. He added, "I do not think we in the West can accept this."[19] Most observers would willingly concede that such a result would be an outrageous crown and conclusion to the efforts of the last fifty years. More than such a conviction will be required, however, to prevent the outcome that the ambassador described as intolerable.

Notes

[1]J. B. Scott, ed., *President Wilson's Foreign Policy* (New York: Oxford University Press, 1918), 191–95.

[2]I. L. Claude, Jr., *Power and International Relations* (New York: Random House, 1967), 123–29.

[3]J. R. Colville, *The Fringes of Power* (London: Hodder and Stoughton, 1985), 563.

[4]J. Erickson, "Total Warfare, 1918–1989," *Scotsman* (Glasgow), 6 February 1993.

[5]J. Joffe, "Collective Security and the Future of Europe: Failed Dreams and Dead Ends," *Survival* 34, no. 1 (1992): 36–37.

[6]The speeches of the Hungarian foreign minister and prime minister are summarized in the *Hungarian Times* (Budapest), 7 June 1993, 1, 4. The same issue of that newspaper contains, on page 2, an article about the fears of Hungarians living in Serbia and, on page 3, a report of a march of protest against the Treaty of Trianon.

[7]Anthony Eden, Earl of Avon, *The Eden Memoirs: Facing the Dictators* (London: Cassell, 1962), 158.

[8]R. G. H. Seitz, *The Montague Burton Lecture* (London: U.S. Information Service, 1992).

[9]*The Diaries of Sir Alexander Cadogan*, ed. D. N. Dilks (London: Cassell, 1971), 790.

[10]*Parliamentary Debates*, Commons, 5th ser., vol. 537 (1 March 1955), col. 1899.

[11]I owe much of the argumentation of this paragraph to R. Langhorne's *The Cold War in Perspective* (Hull: University of Hull Press, 1993).

[12]The speech is reported in the *Daily Telegraph* (London), 1 March 1993.

[13]J. Steinburner, "The Rule of Law," in "Reflections on the New World Order," *Bulletin of the Atomic Scientists* 47, no. 5 (1991): 20.

[14]I am indebted to Lord Home of the Hirsel, foreign secretary at the time, for this information.

[15]Part of the text of President Boris Yeltsin's speech is given in the *Daily Telegraph* (London), 11 November 1992.

[16]Charles A. Kupchan and Clifford A. Kupchan, "Concerts, Collective Security, and the Future of Europe," *International Security* 16, no. 1 (1991): 148–51.

[17]Speech by the Right Honourable Douglas Hurd to the Royal Institute of International Affairs, London, reprinted in the *Daily Telegraph*, 30 January 1993.

[18]G. Flynn and D. J. Scheffer, "Limited Collective Security," *Foreign Policy* 80 (Fall 1990): 83–84.

[19]Seitz, *Montague Burton Lecture*.

Editors and Contributors

STEVEN L. BURG is professor of politics at Brandeis University. He is the author of *Conflict and Cohesion in Socialist Yugoslavia* (1983) and coauthor, with the late Roy C. Macridis, of *Introduction to Comparative Politics: Regimes and Regime Change* (1991). He is also the author of a Twentieth Century Fund study entitled *War or Peace?: Nationalism, Democracy, and American Foreign Policy in Post-Communist Europe* (1996).

MICHAEL BURNS is professor of modern European history at Mount Holyoke College and a former Woodrow Wilson Center fellow. He is the author of *Rural Society and French Politics, 1886–1900* (1984) and *Dreyfus: A Family Affair, 1789–1945* (1991), which won the Best Book Prize of the International Honor Society in History and the Prix Lecache of the Paris-based International League against Racism and Antisemitism (LICRA). Editor of the revised edition of Geoffrey Barraclough's *Main Trends in History* (1991), he has contributed essays to *Living with Antisemitism* (1987) and *Nationhood and Nationalism in France: From Boulangism to the Great War, 1889–1918* (1991).

DAVID N. DILKS is vice-chancellor of the University of Hull, United Kingdom. From 1970 to 1991 he was professor of international history at the University of Leeds and was in 1973 visiting fellow at All Souls' College. Currently president of the International Committee for the History of the Second World War, he has served as research assistant to Sir Anthony Eden, Marshal of the Royal Air Force Lord Tedder, and the Right Honorable Harold Macmillan. He is the author of *Curzon in India* (2 vols.) (1969 and 1970) and *The Missing Dimension* (1984) and the editor of *The Diaries of Sir Alexander Cadogan* (1972), *Retreat from Power* (2 vols.) (1981), *Neville Chamberlain* (vol. 1) (1984),

Barbarossa 1941: The Axis, the Allies, and World War—Retrospect, Recollection, Revision (1994), and *Grossbritannien und der deutsche Wiederstand* (1994).

G. JOHN IKENBERRY is associate professor of political science at the University of Pennsylvania and co-director of the Lauder Institute of Management and International Studies. He is the author of *Reasons of State: Oil Politics and the Capacities of the American Government* (1988) and the coauthor, with John A. Hall, of *The State* (1989). He edited *American Foreign Policy: Theoretical Essays* (1989; 2d ed., 1994) and *The State and American Foreign Economic Policy* (1988). He is currently writing a book about postwar settlements and order creation after major wars.

CHARLES S. MAIER is Krupp Foundation Professor of European Studies, director of the Center for European Studies, and a member of the Department of History at Harvard University. His publications include *Recasting Bourgeois Europe: Stabilization in France, Germany, and Italy in the Decade after World War I* (1975), *In Search of Stability: Explorations in Historical Political Economy* (1987), and *The Unmasterable Past: History, Holocaust, and German National Identity* (1988). His current study of the collapse of the German Democratic Republic and German unification, *Dissolution: The End of East Germany*, will be published in 1997.

ERNEST R. MAY is Charles Warren Professor of History at Harvard University. He has been a consultant to the Joint Chiefs of Staff, the Office of the Secretary of Defense, and the National Security Council and is currently on the board of visitors of the Joint Military Intelligence College. He has served as dean of Harvard College, associate dean of the Faculty of Arts and Sciences, director of the Institute of Politics, and chair of the Department of History. His recent publications include *The Making of the Monroe Doctrine* (1975), *Careers for Humanists* (1981), *Knowing One's Enemies: Intelligence Assessment before the Two World Wars* (1984), and *American Cold War Strategy: Interpreting NSC 68* (1993). He is also coauthor, with Richard E. Neustand, of *Thinking in Time: The Uses of History for Decision-Makers* (1986).

PAULA BAILEY SMITH is program associate for East European Studies, Woodrow Wilson International Center for Scholars. She received a Master of Arts degree with distinction in international relations, concentrating in Soviet studies and international economics, from the Paul H. Nitze School of Advanced International Studies of Johns Hopkins University. She coedited *East European Studies in the United States: Making Its Own Transition after 1989* (1993), was staff editor, with John R. Lampe and Daniel N. Nelson, of *East European Security Reconsidered* (1993), and is the editor of the *East European Studies Newsletter*.

SAMUEL F. WELLS, JR., is deputy director of the Woodrow Wilson International Center for Scholars, and director, West European Studies. He is the author of *The Challenges of Power: American Diplomacy, 1900–1921* (1990) and numerous articles on European-American relations and security affairs. He is the editor of *Economics and World Power: An Assessment of American Diplomacy since 1789* (1984), *Strategic Defenses and Soviet-American Relations* (1987), and *The Helsinki Process and the Future of Europe* (1990).

Index

Page numbers in italics refer to tables.